Official Notary Journal

Book # _____

This Records Notarial Acts
From: ____/____/_____   **To**: ____/____/_____

Notary Printed Name:
Official Signature:
Address:
City: **State:**   **Zip:**
Business Phone: **Other Phone:**
Email Address:
Date of Commission: **Expires:**
Commission #
Jurisdiction:
Bonding Company:
Address:
City: **State:**   **Zip:**
Phone #:
Notes or Other Information:

D1104937

Notary Entry # 1

Date/Time:	_____ / _____ / _____ _____ am / pm
Location:	
Fee: $_____ Travel: _____	

Type of Service

☐ Acknowledgment   ☐ Jurat
☐ Oath/Affirmation   ☐ Certification
☐ Other: _____   Document Date: _____
Document Type: _____

Individual

Printed Name:	
Address:	

Phone # / Email: _____ _____

Signature:

Identification	Witness #1

Identification		Witness #1
☐ Individual	☐ Credible Witness	Printed Name:
☐ Known Personally ☐ Passport ☐ Driver's License ☐ ID Card Other: _____		Address:
ID #: _____ Issued by: _____ Issued On: _____ Expires: _____		Phone or Email: _____ Signature:
		Witness #2
Thumbprint	Thumbprint	Printed Name:
		Address:
		Phone or Email:
		Signature:

Notary Entry #2

Date/Time:	_____/_____/_____ _____ am / pm
Location:	
Fee: $_____ Travel: _____	

Type of Service

☐ Acknowledgment   ☐ Jurat
☐ Oath/Affirmation   ☐ Certification
☐ Other: _____   Document Date: _____
Document Type: _____

Individual Signing

Printed Name:	
Address:	
Phone # / Email: _____ _____	
Signature:	

Identification	Witness #1
☐ Individual ☐ Credible Witness	Printed Name:
☐ Known Personally ☐ Passport ☐ Driver's License ☐ ID Card Other: _____	Address:
ID #: _____ Issued by: _____ Issued On: _____	Phone or Email:
Expires: _____	Signature:
	Witness #2
Thumbprint Thumbprint	Printed Name:
	Address:
	Phone or Email:
	Signature:

Notary Entry #3

Date/Time:	_____/_____/_____ ____ am / pm
Location:	
Fee: $_____ Travel: _____	

Type of Service

☐ Acknowledgment   ☐ Jurat
☐ Oath/Affirmation   ☐ Certification
☐ Other: _____   Document Date: _____
Document Type: _____

Individual

Printed Name:	
Address:	

Phone # / Email: _____ _____

Signature:

Identification		Witness #1	
☐ Individual	☐ Credible Witness	Printed Name:	
☐ Known Personally ☐ Passport		Address:	
☐ Driver's License ☐ ID Card			
Other: _____			
ID #: _____		Phone or Email:	
Issued by: _____			
Issued On: _____		Signature:	
Expires: _____		**Witness #2**	
Thumbprint	Thumbprint	Printed Name:	
		Address:	
		Phone or Email:	
		Signature:	

Notary Entry # 4

Date/Time:	_____/_____/_____ _____ am / pm
Location:	
Fee: $_____ Travel: _____	

Type of Service

☐ Acknowledgment   ☐ Jurat
☐ Oath/Affirmation   ☐ Certification
☐ Other: _____
        Document Date: _____
Document Type: _____

Individual Signing

Printed Name:	
Address:	
Phone # / Email: _____ _____	
Signature:	

Identification	Witness #1
☐ Individual ☐ Credible Witness	Printed Name:
☐ Known Personally ☐ Passport ☐ Driver's License ☐ ID Card Other: _____	Address:
ID #: _____ Issued by: _____ Issued On: _____ Expires: _____	Phone or Email:
	Signature:
	Witness #2
	Printed Name:
Thumbprint Thumbprint	Address:
	Phone or Email:
	Signature:

Notary Entry # 5

Date/Time:	_____/_____/_____ _____ am / pm
Location:	
Fee: $_____ Travel: _____	

Type of Service

☐ Acknowledgment   ☐ Jurat

☐ Oath/Affirmation   ☐ Certification

☐ Other: _____   Document Date: _____

Document Type: _____

Individual

Printed Name:	
Address:	
Phone # / Email: _____ _____	
Signature:	

Identification	Witness #1
☐ Individual ☐ Credible Witness	Printed Name:
☐ Known Personally ☐ Passport ☐ Driver's License ☐ ID Card Other: _____ ID #: _____ Issued by: _____ Issued On: _____ Expires: _____	Address:
	Phone or Email:
	Signature:
	Witness #2
Thumbprint Thumbprint	Printed Name:
	Address:
	Phone or Email:
	Signature:

Notary Entry # 6

Date/Time:	_____ / _____ / _____ _____ am / pm
Location:	
Fee: $_____ Travel: _____	

Type of Service

☐ Acknowledgment   ☐ Jurat
☐ Oath/Affirmation   ☐ Certification
☐ Other: _____   Document Date: _____
Document Type: _____

Individual Signing

Printed Name:	
Address:	

Phone # / Email: _____ _____

Signature:

Identification	Witness #1
☐ Individual ☐ Credible Witness	Printed Name:
☐ Known Personally ☐ Passport ☐ Driver's License ☐ ID Card Other: _____	Address:
ID #: _____ Issued by: _____ Issued On: _____ Expires: _____	Phone or Email: Signature:
	Witness #2
Thumbprint Thumbprint	Printed Name:
	Address:
	Phone or Email:
	Signature:

Notary Entry # 7

Date/Time:	_____/_____/_____ _____ am / pm
Location:	
Fee: $_____	Travel: _____

Type of Service

☐ Acknowledgment   ☐ Jurat

☐ Oath/Affirmation   ☐ Certification

☐ Other: _____   Document Date: _____

Document Type: _____

Individual

Printed Name:	
Address:	
Phone # / Email: _____ _____	
Signature:	

Identification	Witness #1
☐ Individual ☐ Credible Witness	Printed Name:
☐ Known Personally ☐ Passport ☐ Driver's License ☐ ID Card Other: _____	Address:
ID #: _____ Issued by: _____ Issued On: _____ Expires: _____	Phone or Email:
	Signature:
	Witness #2
Thumbprint Thumbprint	Printed Name:
	Address:
	Phone or Email:
	Signature:

Notary Entry #8

Date/Time: _____ / _____ / _____ _____ am / pm

Location:

Fee: $_____ Travel: _____

Type of Service

- ☐ Acknowledgment
- ☐ Oath/Affirmation
- ☐ Other: _____

- ☐ Jurat
- ☐ Certification

Document Date: _____

Document Type: _____

Individual Signing

Printed Name:

Address:

Phone # / Email: _____ _____

Signature:

Identification		Witness #1
☐ Individual ☐ Credible Witness		Printed Name:
☐ Known Personally ☐ Passport ☐ Driver's License ☐ ID Card Other: _____ ID #: _____ Issued by: _____ Issued On: _____ Expires: _____		Address: Phone or Email: Signature:

		Witness #2
Thumbprint	Thumbprint	Printed Name:
		Address:
		Phone or Email:
		Signature:

Notary Entry #9

Date/Time:	_____/_____/_____ _____ am / pm
Location:	
Fee: $_____ Travel: _____	

Type of Service

☐ Acknowledgment   ☐ Jurat
☐ Oath/Affirmation   ☐ Certification
☐ Other: _____   Document Date: _____
Document Type: _____

Individual

Printed Name:	
Address:	
Phone # / Email: _____ _____	
Signature:	

Identification	Witness #1
☐ Individual ☐ Credible Witness	Printed Name:
☐ Known Personally ☐ Passport ☐ Driver's License ☐ ID Card Other: _____ ID #: _____ Issued by: _____	Address:
	Phone or Email:
Issued On: _____ Expires: _____	Signature:
	Witness #2
Thumbprint Thumbprint	Printed Name:
	Address:
	Phone or Email:
	Signature:

Notary Entry #10

Date/Time:	____ / ____ / _____ ____ am / pm
Location:	
Fee: $_____	Travel: _____

Type of Service

☐ Acknowledgment   ☐ Jurat

☐ Oath/Affirmation   ☐ Certification

☐ Other: _____   Document Date: _____

Document Type: _____

Individual Signing

Printed Name:	
Address:	
Phone # / Email:	_____ _____
Signature:	

Identification	Witness #1

Identification	Witness #1
☐ Individual ☐ Credible Witness	Printed Name:
☐ Known Personally ☐ Passport ☐ Driver's License ☐ ID Card Other: _____	Address:
ID #: _____ Issued by: _____ Issued On: _____ Expires: _____	Phone or Email: Signature:

		Witness #2
Thumbprint	Thumbprint	Printed Name:
		Address:
		Phone or Email:
		Signature:

Notary Entry #11

Date/Time: _____/_____/_____ _____ am / pm

Location:

Fee: $_____   Travel: _____

Type of Service

☐ Acknowledgment   ☐ Jurat
☐ Oath/Affirmation   ☐ Certification
☐ Other: _____   Document Date: _____
Document Type: _____

Individual

Printed Name:

Address:

Phone # / Email: _____ _____

Signature:

Identification		Witness #1
☐ Individual	☐ Credible Witness	Printed Name:
☐ Known Personally ☐ Passport		Address:
☐ Driver's License ☐ ID Card		
Other: _____		
ID #: _____		Phone or Email:
Issued by: _____		
Issued On: _____		Signature:
Expires: _____		**Witness #2**
Thumbprint	Thumbprint	Printed Name:
		Address:
		Phone or Email:
		Signature:

Notary Entry #12

Date/Time:	_____ / _____ / _____ _____ am / pm
Location:	
Fee: $_____ Travel: _____	

Type of Service

☐ Acknowledgment   ☐ Jurat
☐ Oath/Affirmation   ☐ Certification
☐ Other: _____   Document Date: _____
Document Type: _____

Individual Signing

Printed Name:	
Address:	
Phone # / Email: _____ _____	
Signature:	

Identification | Witness #1

Identification	Witness #1
☐ Individual ☐ Credible Witness	Printed Name:
☐ Known Personally ☐ Passport ☐ Driver's License ☐ ID Card Other: _____ ID #: _____ Issued by: _____ Issued On: _____ Expires: _____	Address:
	Phone or Email:
	Signature:

Witness #2

Thumbprint	Thumbprint	
		Printed Name:
		Address:
		Phone or Email:
		Signature:

Notary Entry #13

Date/Time:	_____ / _____ / _____ _____ am / pm
Location:	
Fee: $_____ Travel: _____	

Type of Service

☐ Acknowledgment ☐ Jurat
☐ Oath/Affirmation ☐ Certification
☐ Other: _____ Document Date: _____
Document Type: _____

Individual

Printed Name:	
Address:	

Phone # / Email: _____ _____

Signature:

Identification	Witness #1
☐ Individual ☐ Credible Witness	Printed Name:
☐ Known Personally ☐ Passport ☐ Driver's License ☐ ID Card Other: _____ ID #: _____ Issued by: _____ Issued On: _____ Expires: _____	Address:
	Phone or Email:
	Signature:
	Witness #2
Thumbprint	Thumbprint	Printed Name:
	Address:
	Phone or Email:
	Signature:

Notary Entry # 14

Date/Time:	_____ / _____ / _____ _____ am / pm
Location:	
Fee: $_____	Travel: _____

Type of Service

☐ Acknowledgment   ☐ Jurat
☐ Oath/Affirmation   ☐ Certification
☐ Other: _____   Document Date: _____
Document Type: _____

Individual Signing

Printed Name:	
Address:	
Phone # / Email:	_____ _____
Signature:	

Identification		**Witness #1**
☐ Individual	☐ Credible Witness	Printed Name:
☐ Known Personally	☐ Passport	Address:
☐ Driver's License	☐ ID Card	
Other: _____		
ID #: _____		Phone or Email:
Issued by: _____		
Issued On: _____		Signature:
Expires: _____		**Witness #2**
Thumbprint	Thumbprint	Printed Name:
		Address:
		Phone or Email:
		Signature:

Notary Entry #15

Date/Time: _____/_____/_____ _____ am / pm

Location:

Fee: $_____   Travel: _____

Type of Service

☐ Acknowledgment   ☐ Jurat
☐ Oath/Affirmation   ☐ Certification
☐ Other: _____   Document Date: _____
Document Type: _____

Individual

Printed Name:

Address:

Phone # / Email: _____ _____

Signature:

Identification		Witness #1
☐ Individual	☐ Credible Witness	Printed Name:
☐ Known Personally ☐ Passport		Address:
☐ Driver's License ☐ ID Card		
Other: _____		
ID #: _____		Phone or Email:
Issued by: _____		
Issued On: _____		Signature:
Expires: _____		**Witness #2**
Thumbprint	Thumbprint	Printed Name:
		Address:
		Phone or Email:
		Signature:

Notary Entry #16

Date/Time:	_____/_____/_____ _____ am / pm
Location:	
Fee: $_____	Travel: _____

Type of Service

☐ Acknowledgment   ☐ Jurat

☐ Oath/Affirmation   ☐ Certification

☐ Other: _____

Document Date: _____

Document Type: _____

Individual Signing

Printed Name:	
Address:	

Phone # / Email: _____ _____

Signature:

Identification		Witness #1
☐ Individual	☐ Credible Witness	**Printed Name:**
☐ Known Personally	☐ Passport	**Address:**
☐ Driver's License	☐ ID Card	
Other: _____		
ID #: _____		**Phone or Email:**
Issued by: _____		
Issued On: _____		Signature:
Expires: _____		**Witness #2**
Thumbprint	Thumbprint	**Printed Name:**
		Address:
		Phone or Email:
		Signature:

Notary Entry #17

Date/Time:	_____ / _____ / _____ _____ am / pm
Location:	
Fee: $_____ Travel: _____	

Type of Service

☐ Acknowledgment   ☐ Jurat
☐ Oath/Affirmation   ☐ Certification
☐ Other: _____   Document Date: _____

Document Type: _____

Individual

Printed Name:	
Address:	

Phone # / Email: _____ _____

Signature:

Identification	Witness #1
☐ Individual ☐ Credible Witness	Printed Name:
☐ Known Personally ☐ Passport	Address:
☐ Driver's License ☐ ID Card	
Other: _____	
ID #: _____	Phone or Email:
Issued by: _____	
Issued On: _____	Signature:
Expires: _____	Witness #2
Thumbprint	Thumbprint	Printed Name:
		Address:
		Phone or Email:
		Signature:

Notary Entry #18

Date/Time:	_____ / _____ / _____ _____ am / pm
Location:	
Fee: $_____ Travel: _____	

Type of Service

☐ Acknowledgment   ☐ Jurat
☐ Oath/Affirmation   ☐ Certification
☐ Other: _____   Document Date: _____
Document Type: _____

Individual Signing

Printed Name:	
Address:	

Phone # / Email: _____ _____

Signature:

Identification	Witness #1
☐ Individual ☐ Credible Witness	Printed Name:
☐ Known Personally ☐ Passport	Address:
☐ Driver's License ☐ ID Card	
Other: _____	
ID #: _____	Phone or Email:
Issued by: _____	
Issued On: _____	Signature:
Expires: _____	**Witness #2**
Thumbprint Thumbprint	Printed Name:
	Address:
	Phone or Email:
	Signature:

Notary Entry # 19

Date/Time: _____ / _____ / _____ _____ am / pm

Location:

Fee: $_____   Travel: _____

Type of Service

☐ Acknowledgment   ☐ Jurat

☐ Oath/Affirmation   ☐ Certification

☐ Other: _____   Document Date: _____

Document Type: _____

Individual

Printed Name:

Address:

Phone # / Email: _____ _____

Signature:

Identification		Witness #1
☐ Individual	☐ Credible Witness	Printed Name:
☐ Known Personally ☐ Passport ☐ Driver's License ☐ ID Card		Address:
Other: _____ ID #: _____ Issued by: _____ Issued On: _____ Expires: _____		Phone or Email:
		Signature:
		Witness #2
Thumbprint	Thumbprint	Printed Name:
		Address:
		Phone or Email:
		Signature:

Notary Entry #20

Date/Time:	_____ / _____ / _____ _____ am / pm
Location:	
Fee: $_____ Travel: _____	

Type of Service

☐ Acknowledgment   ☐ Jurat
☐ Oath/Affirmation   ☐ Certification
☐ Other: _____   Document Date: _____
Document Type: _____

Individual Signing

Printed Name:	
Address:	
Phone # / Email: _____ _____	
Signature:	

Identification	Witness #1
☐ Individual ☐ Credible Witness	Printed Name:
☐ Known Personally ☐ Passport ☐ Driver's License ☐ ID Card Other: _____	Address:
ID #: _____ Issued by: _____	Phone or Email:
Issued On: _____ Expires: _____	Signature:
	Witness #2
Thumbprint Thumbprint	Printed Name:
	Address:
	Phone or Email:
	Signature:

Notary Entry # 21

Date/Time:	_____ / _____ / _____ _____ am / pm
Location:	
Fee: $_____ Travel: _____	

Type of Service

☐ Acknowledgment   ☐ Jurat
☐ Oath/Affirmation   ☐ Certification
☐ Other: _____ Document Date: _____
Document Type: _____

Individual

Printed Name:	
Address:	

Phone # / Email: _____ _____

Signature:

Identification	Witness #1

☐ Individual	☐ Credible Witness	Printed Name:
☐ Known Personally ☐ Passport		Address:
☐ Driver's License ☐ ID Card		
Other: _____		
ID #: _____		Phone or Email:
Issued by: _____		
Issued On: _____		Signature:
Expires: _____		

		Witness #2
		Printed Name:
Thumbprint	Thumbprint	Address:
		Phone or Email:
		Signature:

Notary Entry # 22

Date/Time:	_____/_____/_____ _____ am / pm
Location:	
Fee: $_____ Travel: _____	

Type of Service

☐ Acknowledgment   ☐ Jurat
☐ Oath/Affirmation   ☐ Certification
☐ Other: _____   Document Date: _____
Document Type: _____

Individual Signing

Printed Name:	
Address:	
Phone # / Email: _____ _____	
Signature:	

Identification / Witness #1

Identification		Witness #1
☐ Individual	☐ Credible Witness	Printed Name:
☐ Known Personally ☐ Passport		Address:
☐ Driver's License ☐ ID Card		
Other: _____		
ID #: _____		Phone or Email:
Issued by: _____		
Issued On: _____		Signature:
Expires: _____		Witness #2
Thumbprint	Thumbprint	Printed Name:
		Address:
		Phone or Email:
		Signature:

Notary Entry #23

Date/Time:	____/____/_____ _____ am / pm
Location:	
Fee: $_____ Travel: _____	

Type of Service

☐ Acknowledgment   ☐ Jurat
☐ Oath/Affirmation   ☐ Certification
☐ Other: _____   Document Date: _____
Document Type: _____

Individual

Printed Name:	
Address:	
Phone # / Email: _____ _____	
Signature:	

Identification	Witness #1

Identification		Witness #1
☐ Individual	☐ Credible Witness	Printed Name:
☐ Known Personally ☐ Passport ☐ Driver's License ☐ ID Card Other: _____		Address:
ID #: _____ Issued by: _____		Phone or Email:
Issued On: _____		Signature:
Expires: _____		**Witness #2**
Thumbprint	Thumbprint	Printed Name:
		Address:
		Phone or Email:
		Signature:

Notary Entry #24

Date/Time:	_____/_____/_____ _____ am / pm
Location:	
Fee: $_____	Travel: _____

Type of Service

☐ Acknowledgment   ☐ Jurat

☐ Oath/Affirmation   ☐ Certification

☐ Other: _____   Document Date: _____

Document Type: _____

Individual Signing

Printed Name:	
Address:	

Phone # / Email: _____ _____

Signature:

Identification	Witness #1

☐ Individual	☐ Credible Witness	Printed Name:
☐ Known Personally ☐ Passport		Address:
☐ Driver's License ☐ ID Card		
Other: _____		
ID #: _____		Phone or Email:
Issued by: _____		
Issued On: _____		Signature:
Expires: _____		

	Witness #2

Thumbprint	Thumbprint	Printed Name:
		Address:
		Phone or Email:
		Signature:

Notary Entry #25

Date/Time:	_____ / _____ / _____ _____ am / pm
Location:	
Fee: $_____ Travel: _____	

Type of Service

☐ Acknowledgment   ☐ Jurat
☐ Oath/Affirmation   ☐ Certification
☐ Other: _____   Document Date: _____

Document Type: _____

Individual

Printed Name:	
Address:	

Phone # / Email: _____ _____

Signature:

Identification	Witness #1
☐ Individual ☐ Credible Witness	Printed Name:
☐ Known Personally ☐ Passport ☐ Driver's License ☐ ID Card Other: _____ ID #: _____ Issued by: _____ Issued On: _____	Address:
	Phone or Email:
Expires: _____	Signature:

Identification (cont.)	Witness #2
	Printed Name:
Thumbprint Thumbprint	Address:
	Phone or Email:
	Signature:

Notary Entry # 26

Date/Time:	_____/_____/_____ _____ am / pm
Location:	
Fee: $_____	Travel: _____

Type of Service

☐ Acknowledgment   ☐ Jurat
☐ Oath/Affirmation   ☐ Certification
☐ Other: _____   Document Date: _____
Document Type: _____

Individual Signing

Printed Name:	
Address:	
Phone # / Email: _____ _____	
Signature:	

Identification		Witness #1
☐ Individual	☐ Credible Witness	Printed Name:
☐ Known Personally	☐ Passport	Address:
☐ Driver's License	☐ ID Card	
Other: _____		
ID #: _____		Phone or Email:
Issued by: _____		
Issued On: _____		Signature:
Expires: _____		Witness #2
Thumbprint	Thumbprint	Printed Name:
		Address:
		Phone or Email:
		Signature:

Notary Entry # 27

Date/Time:	____ / ____ / _____ _____ am / pm
Location:	
Fee: $_____ Travel: _____	

Type of Service

☐ Acknowledgment   ☐ Jurat
☐ Oath/Affirmation   ☐ Certification
☐ Other: _____   Document Date: _____
Document Type: _____

Individual

Printed Name:	
Address:	

Phone # / Email: _____ _____

Signature:

Identification	Witness #1
☐ Individual ☐ Credible Witness	Printed Name:
☐ Known Personally ☐ Passport ☐ Driver's License ☐ ID Card	Address:
Other: _____	
ID #: _____	Phone or Email:
Issued by: _____	
Issued On: _____	Signature:
Expires: _____	**Witness #2**

Thumbprint	Thumbprint	Printed Name:
		Address:
		Phone or Email:
		Signature:

Notary Entry #28

Date/Time:	___/___/_____ _____ am / pm
Location:	
Fee: $_____ Travel: _____	

Type of Service

☐ Acknowledgment   ☐ Jurat
☐ Oath/Affirmation   ☐ Certification
☐ Other: _____   Document Date: _____
Document Type: _____

Individual Signing

Printed Name:	
Address:	
Phone # / Email: _____ _____	
Signature:	

Identification	Witness #1
☐ Individual ☐ Credible Witness	Printed Name:
☐ Known Personally ☐ Passport	Address:
☐ Driver's License ☐ ID Card	
Other: _____	
ID #: _____	Phone or Email:
Issued by: _____	
Issued On: _____	Signature:
Expires: _____	**Witness #2**
	Printed Name:
Thumbprint Thumbprint	Address:
	Phone or Email:
	Signature:

Notary Entry #29

Date/Time:	_____/_____/_____ _____ am / pm
Location:	
Fee: $_____	Travel: _____

Type of Service

☐ Acknowledgment   ☐ Jurat
☐ Oath/Affirmation   ☐ Certification
☐ Other: _____   Document Date: _____
Document Type: _____

Individual

Printed Name:	
Address:	

Phone # / Email: _____ _____

Signature:

Identification	Witness #1

☐ Individual	☐ Credible Witness	Printed Name:
☐ Known Personally ☐ Passport		Address:
☐ Driver's License ☐ ID Card		
Other: _____		
ID #: _____		Phone or Email:
Issued by: _____		
Issued On: _____		Signature:
Expires: _____		**Witness #2**

		Printed Name:
Thumbprint	Thumbprint	Address:
		Phone or Email:
		Signature:

Notary Entry #30

Date/Time:	_____/_____/_____ _____ am / pm
Location:	

Fee: $_____   Travel: _____

Type of Service

☐ Acknowledgment   ☐ Jurat
☐ Oath/Affirmation   ☐ Certification
☐ Other: _____ Document Date: _____
Document Type: _____

Individual Signing

Printed Name:	
Address:	

Phone # / Email: _____ _____

Signature:

Identification	Witness #1
☐ Individual ☐ Credible Witness	Printed Name:
☐ Known Personally ☐ Passport	Address:
☐ Driver's License ☐ ID Card	
Other: _____	
ID #: _____	Phone or Email:
Issued by: _____	
Issued On: _____	Signature:
Expires: _____	**Witness #2**
	Printed Name:
Thumbprint Thumbprint	Address:
	Phone or Email:
	Signature:

Notary Entry #31

Date/Time:	_____ / _____ / _____ _____ am / pm
Location:	

Fee: $_____   Travel: _____

Type of Service

☐ Acknowledgment   ☐ Jurat
☐ Oath/Affirmation   ☐ Certification
☐ Other: _____   Document Date: _____
Document Type: _____

Individual

Printed Name:	
Address:	

Phone # / Email: _____ _____

Signature:

Identification	Witness #1

Identification

☐ Individual   ☐ Credible Witness

☐ Known Personally ☐ Passport
☐ Driver's License   ☐ ID Card
    Other: _____
ID #: _____
Issued by: _____
Issued On: _____
Expires: _____

Witness #1
Printed Name:
Address:
Phone or Email:
Signature:

Witness #2
Printed Name:
Address:
Phone or Email:
Signature:

Thumbprint	Thumbprint

Notary Entry #32

Date/Time:	_____ / _____ / _____ _____ am / pm
Location:	

Fee: $_____   Travel: _____

Type of Service

☐ Acknowledgment   ☐ Jurat
☐ Oath/Affirmation   ☐ Certification
☐ Other: _____   Document Date: _____
Document Type: _____

Individual Signing

Printed Name:	
Address:	

Phone # / Email: _____ _____

Signature:

Identification	Witness #1
☐ Individual ☐ Credible Witness	Printed Name:
☐ Known Personally ☐ Passport	Address:
☐ Driver's License ☐ ID Card	
Other: _____	
ID #: _____	Phone or Email:
Issued by: _____	
Issued On: _____	Signature:
Expires: _____	**Witness #2**
	Printed Name:
Thumbprint Thumbprint	Address:
	Phone or Email:
	Signature:

Notary Entry #33

Date/Time:	_____/_____/_____ _____ am / pm
Location:	
Fee: $_____ Travel: _____	

Type of Service

☐ Acknowledgment   ☐ Jurat

☐ Oath/Affirmation   ☐ Certification

☐ Other: _____   Document Date: _____

Document Type: _____

Individual

Printed Name:	
Address:	

Phone # / Email: _____ _____

Signature:

Identification	Witness #1
☐ Individual ☐ Credible Witness	Printed Name:
☐ Known Personally ☐ Passport ☐ Driver's License ☐ ID Card	Address:
Other: _____ ID #: _____ Issued by: _____	Phone or Email:
Issued On: _____	Signature:
Expires: _____	**Witness #2**

Thumbprint	Thumbprint	Printed Name:
		Address:
		Phone or Email:
		Signature:

Notary Entry #34

Date/Time:	_____/_____/_____ _____ am / pm
Location:	
Fee: $_____	Travel: _____

Type of Service

☐ Acknowledgment   ☐ Jurat

☐ Oath/Affirmation   ☐ Certification

☐ Other: _____   Document Date: _____

Document Type: _____

Individual Signing

Printed Name:	
Address:	
Phone # / Email:	_____ _____
Signature:	

Identification	Witness #1

Identification		Witness #1
☐ Individual	☐ Credible Witness	Printed Name:
☐ Known Personally	☐ Passport	Address:
☐ Driver's License	☐ ID Card	
Other: _____		Phone or Email:
ID #: _____		
Issued by: _____		Signature:
Issued On: _____		**Witness #2**
Expires: _____		Printed Name:
Thumbprint	Thumbprint	Address:
		Phone or Email:
		Signature:

Notary Entry #35

Date/Time: _____/_____/_____ _____ am / pm

Location:

Fee: $_____ Travel: _____

Type of Service

☐ Acknowledgment   ☐ Jurat
☐ Oath/Affirmation   ☐ Certification
☐ Other: _____   Document Date: _____
Document Type: _____

Individual

Printed Name:

Address:

Phone # / Email: _____ _____

Signature:

Identification		Witness #1
☐ Individual	☐ Credible Witness	Printed Name:
☐ Known Personally ☐ Passport		Address:
☐ Driver's License ☐ ID Card		
Other: _____		
ID #: _____		Phone or Email:
Issued by: _____		
Issued On: _____		Signature:
Expires: _____		Witness #2
Thumbprint	Thumbprint	Printed Name:
		Address:
		Phone or Email:
		Signature:

Notary Entry #36

Date/Time:	_____/_____/_____ _____ am / pm
Location:	
Fee: $_____	Travel: _____

Type of Service

☐ Acknowledgment   ☐ Jurat

☐ Oath/Affirmation   ☐ Certification

☐ Other: _____ Document Date: _____

Document Type: _____

Individual Signing

Printed Name:	
Address:	

Phone # / Email: _____ _____

Signature:

Identification	Witness #1

Identification

☐ Individual   ☐ Credible Witness

☐ Known Personally ☐ Passport

☐ Driver's License ☐ ID Card

Other: _____

ID #: _____

Issued by: _____

Issued On: _____

Expires: _____

Witness #1

Printed Name:

Address:

Phone or Email:

Signature:

Witness #2

Printed Name:

Address:

Phone or Email:

Signature:

Thumbprint	Thumbprint

Notary Entry #37

Date/Time: _____/_____/_____ _____ am / pm

Location:

Fee: $_____   Travel: _____

Type of Service

☐ Acknowledgment   ☐ Jurat
☐ Oath/Affirmation   ☐ Certification
☐ Other: _____   Document Date: _____
Document Type: _____

Individual

Printed Name:

Address:

Phone # / Email: _____ _____

Signature:

Identification	Witness #1
☐ Individual ☐ Credible Witness	Printed Name:
☐ Known Personally ☐ Passport ☐ Driver's License ☐ ID Card Other: _____ ID #: _____ Issued by: _____ Issued On: _____ Expires: _____	Address:
	Phone or Email:
	Signature:
	Witness #2
Thumbprint Thumbprint	Printed Name:
	Address:
	Phone or Email:
	Signature:

Notary Entry #38

Date/Time:	_____ / _____ / _____ _____ am / pm
Location:	
Fee: $_____ Travel: _____	

Type of Service

☐ Acknowledgment   ☐ Jurat
☐ Oath/Affirmation   ☐ Certification
☐ Other: _____   Document Date: _____
Document Type: _____

Individual Signing

Printed Name:	
Address:	
Phone # / Email: _____ _____	
Signature:	

Identification

☐ Individual	☐ Credible Witness

☐ Known Personally ☐ Passport
☐ Driver's License ☐ ID Card
   Other: _____
ID #: _____
Issued by: _____
Issued On: _____
Expires: _____

Thumbprint	Thumbprint

Witness #1

Printed Name:
Address:

Phone or Email:
Signature:

Witness #2

Printed Name:
Address:

Phone or Email:
Signature:

Notary Entry # 39

Date/Time:	_____/_____/_____ _____ am / pm
Location:	
Fee: $_____ Travel: _____	

Type of Service

☐ Acknowledgment   ☐ Jurat
☐ Oath/Affirmation   ☐ Certification
☐ Other: _____   Document Date: _____
Document Type: _____

Individual

Printed Name:	
Address:	

Phone # / Email: _____ _____

Signature:

Identification	Witness #1

Identification		Witness #1
☐ Individual ☐ Credible Witness		Printed Name:
☐ Known Personally ☐ Passport ☐ Driver's License ☐ ID Card Other: _____ ID #: _____ Issued by: _____ Issued On: _____ Expires: _____		Address:
		Phone or Email:
		Signature:

Witness #2

Thumbprint	Thumbprint	Printed Name:
		Address:
		Phone or Email:
		Signature:

Notary Entry #40

Date/Time:	____ / ____ / _____ ____ am / pm
Location:	
Fee: $_____ Travel: _____	

Type of Service

☐ Acknowledgment   ☐ Jurat
☐ Oath/Affirmation   ☐ Certification
☐ Other: _____   Document Date: _____
Document Type: _____

Individual Signing

Printed Name:	
Address:	
Phone # / Email: _____ _____	
Signature:	

Identification	Witness #1
☐ Individual ☐ Credible Witness	Printed Name:
☐ Known Personally ☐ Passport ☐ Driver's License ☐ ID Card Other: _____ ID #: _____ Issued by: _____ Issued On: _____ Expires: _____	Address:
	Phone or Email:
	Signature:
	Witness #2
Thumbprint Thumbprint	Printed Name:
	Address:
	Phone or Email:
	Signature:

Notary Entry #41

Date/Time:	_____/_____/_____ _____ am / pm
Location:	
Fee: $_____	Travel: _____

Type of Service

☐ Acknowledgment   ☐ Jurat
☐ Oath/Affirmation   ☐ Certification
☐ Other: _____   Document Date: _____
Document Type: _____

Individual

Printed Name:	
Address:	
Phone # / Email:	_____ _____
Signature:	

Identification	Witness #1
☐ Individual ☐ Credible Witness	Printed Name:
☐ Known Personally ☐ Passport	Address:
☐ Driver's License ☐ ID Card	
Other: _____	
ID #: _____	Phone or Email:
Issued by: _____	
Issued On: _____	Signature:
Expires: _____	**Witness #2**
	Printed Name:
Thumbprint Thumbprint	Address:
	Phone or Email:
	Signature:

Notary Entry #42

Date/Time:	_____/_____/_____ _____ am / pm
Location:	
Fee: $_____ Travel: _____	

Type of Service

☐ Acknowledgment   ☐ Jurat
☐ Oath/Affirmation   ☐ Certification
☐ Other: _____   Document Date: _____
Document Type: _____

Individual Signing

Printed Name:	
Address:	
Phone # / Email: _____ _____	
Signature:	

Identification / Witness #1

Identification

☐ Individual   ☐ Credible Witness
☐ Known Personally   ☐ Passport
☐ Driver's License   ☐ ID Card
     Other: _____
ID #: _____
Issued by: _____
Issued On: _____
Expires: _____

Witness #1

Printed Name:
Address:

Phone or Email:
Signature:

Witness #2

Printed Name:
Address:

Phone or Email:
Signature:

Thumbprint	Thumbprint

Notary Entry #43

Date/Time: _____/_____/_____ _____ am / pm

Location:

Fee: $_____   Travel: _____

Type of Service

☐ Acknowledgment   ☐ Jurat
☐ Oath/Affirmation   ☐ Certification
☐ Other: _____   Document Date: _____
Document Type: _____

Individual

Printed Name:

Address:

Phone # / Email: _____ _____

Signature:

Identification	Witness #1

Identification

☐ Individual   ☐ Credible Witness

☐ Known Personally ☐ Passport
☐ Driver's License ☐ ID Card
  Other: _____
ID #: _____
Issued by: _____
Issued On: _____
Expires: _____

Witness #1

Printed Name:

Address:

Phone or Email:

Signature:

Thumbprint	Thumbprint

Witness #2

Printed Name:

Address:

Phone or Email:

Signature:

Notary Entry # 44

Date/Time:	_____/_____/_____ _____ am / pm
Location:	
Fee: $_____	Travel: _____

Type of Service

☐ Acknowledgment   ☐ Jurat

☐ Oath/Affirmation   ☐ Certification

☐ Other: _____   Document Date: _____

Document Type: _____

Individual Signing

Printed Name:	
Address:	
Phone # / Email:	_____ _____
Signature:	

Identification		Witness #1
☐ Individual	☐ Credible Witness	Printed Name:
☐ Known Personally	☐ Passport	Address:
☐ Driver's License	☐ ID Card	
Other: _____		
ID #: _____		Phone or Email:
Issued by: _____		
Issued On: _____		Signature:
Expires: _____		Witness #2
Thumbprint	Thumbprint	Printed Name:
		Address:
		Phone or Email:
		Signature:

Notary Entry # 45

Date/Time: _____/_____/_____ _____ am / pm

Location:

Fee: $_____   Travel: _____

Type of Service

☐ Acknowledgment   ☐ Jurat
☐ Oath/Affirmation   ☐ Certification
☐ Other: _____   Document Date: _____
Document Type: _____

Individual

Printed Name:

Address:

Phone # / Email: _____ _____

Signature:

Identification	Witness #1
☐ Individual ☐ Credible Witness	Printed Name:
☐ Known Personally ☐ Passport ☐ Driver's License ☐ ID Card Other: _____	Address:
ID #: _____ Issued by: _____ Issued On: _____	Phone or Email:
Expires: _____	Signature:

		Witness #2
Thumbprint	Thumbprint	Printed Name:
		Address:
		Phone or Email:
		Signature:

Notary Entry # 46

Date/Time:	_____/_____/_____ _____ am / pm
Location:	
Fee: $_____	Travel: _____

Type of Service

☐ Acknowledgment   ☐ Jurat
☐ Oath/Affirmation   ☐ Certification
☐ Other: _____   Document Date: _____
Document Type: _____

Individual Signing

Printed Name:	
Address:	

Phone # / Email: _____ _____

Signature:

Identification	Witness #1
☐ Individual ☐ Credible Witness	Printed Name:
☐ Known Personally ☐ Passport	Address:
☐ Driver's License ☐ ID Card	
Other: _____	
ID #: _____	Phone or Email:
Issued by: _____	
Issued On: _____	Signature:
Expires: _____	Witness #2
Thumbprint Thumbprint	Printed Name:
	Address:
	Phone or Email:
	Signature:

Notary Entry #47

Date/Time:	_____ / _____ / _____ _____ am / pm
Location:	
Fee: $_____ Travel: _____	

Type of Service

☐ Acknowledgment   ☐ Jurat
☐ Oath/Affirmation   ☐ Certification
☐ Other: _____ Document Date: _____
Document Type: _____

Individual

Printed Name:	
Address:	

Phone # / Email: _____ _____

Signature:

Identification		Witness #1	

Identification

☐ Individual   ☐ Credible Witness

☐ Known Personally ☐ Passport
☐ Driver's License ☐ ID Card
   Other: _____
ID #: _____
Issued by: _____
Issued On: _____
Expires: _____

Witness #1

Printed Name:

Address:

Phone or Email:

Signature:

Witness #2

Printed Name:

Address:

Phone or Email:

Signature:

Thumbprint	Thumbprint

Notary Entry #48

Date/Time:	_____ / _____ / _____ _____ am / pm
Location:	
Fee: $_____ Travel: _____	

Type of Service

☐ Acknowledgment   ☐ Jurat
☐ Oath/Affirmation   ☐ Certification
☐ Other: _____   Document Date: _____

Document Type: _____

Individual Signing

Printed Name:	
Address:	

Phone # / Email: _____ _____

Signature:

Identification	Witness #1

Identification

☐ Individual   ☐ Credible Witness
☐ Known Personally ☐ Passport
☐ Driver's License ☐ ID Card
   Other: _____
ID #: _____
Issued by: _____
Issued On: _____
Expires: _____

Thumbprint	Thumbprint

Witness #1

Printed Name:
Address:

Phone or Email:
Signature:

Witness #2

Printed Name:
Address:

Phone or Email:
Signature:

Notary Entry #49

Date/Time:	_____ / _____ / _____ _____ am / pm
Location:	
Fee: $_____ Travel: _____	

Type of Service

☐ Acknowledgment   ☐ Jurat
☐ Oath/Affirmation   ☐ Certification
☐ Other: _____   Document Date: _____
Document Type: _____

Individual

Printed Name:	
Address:	

Phone # / Email: _____ _____

Signature:

Identification	Witness #1
☐ Individual ☐ Credible Witness	Printed Name:
☐ Known Personally ☐ Passport ☐ Driver's License ☐ ID Card	Address:
Other: _____ ID #: _____ Issued by: _____ Issued On: _____	Phone or Email:
Expires: _____	Signature:
	Witness #2
Thumbprint Thumbprint	Printed Name:
	Address:
	Phone or Email:
	Signature:

Notary Entry #50

Date/Time:	_____/_____/_____ _____ am / pm
Location:	
Fee: $_____ Travel: _____	

Type of Service

☐ Acknowledgment   ☐ Jurat
☐ Oath/Affirmation   ☐ Certification
☐ Other: _____   Document Date: _____
Document Type: _____

Individual Signing

Printed Name:	
Address:	
Phone # / Email: _____ _____	
Signature:	

Identification		Witness #1
☐ Individual	☐ Credible Witness	Printed Name:
☐ Known Personally ☐ Passport		Address:
☐ Driver's License ☐ ID Card		
Other: _____		
ID #: _____		Phone or Email:
Issued by: _____		
Issued On: _____		Signature:
Expires: _____		**Witness #2**
		Printed Name:
Thumbprint	Thumbprint	Address:
		Phone or Email:
		Signature:

Notary Entry #51

Date/Time:	_____ / _____ / _____ _____ am / pm
Location:	
Fee: $_____	Travel: _____

Type of Service

☐ Acknowledgment   ☐ Jurat

☐ Oath/Affirmation   ☐ Certification

☐ Other: _____   Document Date: _____

Document Type: _____

Individual

Printed Name:	
Address:	

Phone # / Email: _____ _____

Signature:

Identification	Witness #1

Identification		Witness #1
☐ Individual ☐ Credible Witness		Printed Name:
☐ Known Personally ☐ Passport		Address:
☐ Driver's License ☐ ID Card		
Other: _____		
ID #: _____		Phone or Email:
Issued by: _____		
Issued On: _____		Signature:
Expires: _____		Witness #2
Thumbprint	Thumbprint	Printed Name:
		Address:
		Phone or Email:
		Signature:

Notary Entry #52

Date/Time:	_____/_____/_____ _____ am / pm
Location:	
Fee: $_____ Travel: _____	

Type of Service

☐ Acknowledgment   ☐ Jurat
☐ Oath/Affirmation   ☐ Certification
☐ Other: _____   Document Date: _____
Document Type: _____

Individual Signing

Printed Name:	
Address:	
Phone # / Email: _____ _____	
Signature:	

Identification	Witness #1
☐ Individual ☐ Credible Witness	Printed Name:
☐ Known Personally ☐ Passport ☐ Driver's License ☐ ID Card	Address:
Other: _____	
ID #: _____	Phone or Email:
Issued by: _____	
Issued On: _____	Signature:
Expires: _____	**Witness #2**
	Printed Name:
Thumbprint Thumbprint	Address:
	Phone or Email:
	Signature:

Notary Entry #53

Date/Time:	____/____/_____ ____ am / pm
Location:	

Fee: $_____ Travel: _____

Type of Service

☐ Acknowledgment   ☐ Jurat
☐ Oath/Affirmation   ☐ Certification
☐ Other: _____   Document Date: _____
Document Type: _____

Individual

Printed Name:	
Address:	

Phone # / Email: _____ _____

Signature:

Identification		Witness #1
☐ Individual	☐ Credible Witness	Printed Name:
☐ Known Personally ☐ Passport ☐ Driver's License ☐ ID Card		Address:
Other: _____ ID #: _____ Issued by: _____ Issued On: _____ Expires: _____		Phone or Email:
		Signature:
		Witness #2
Thumbprint	Thumbprint	Printed Name:
		Address:
		Phone or Email:
		Signature:

Notary Entry #54

Date/Time:	_____/_____/_____ _____ am / pm
Location:	
Fee: $_____ Travel: _____	

Type of Service

☐ Acknowledgment   ☐ Jurat

☐ Oath/Affirmation   ☐ Certification

☐ Other: _____   Document Date: _____

Document Type: _____

Individual Signing

Printed Name:	
Address:	
Phone # / Email: _____ _____	
Signature:	

Identification	Witness #1

☐ Individual	☐ Credible Witness	Printed Name:
☐ Known Personally ☐ Passport		Address:
☐ Driver's License ☐ ID Card		
Other: _____		
ID #: _____		Phone or Email:
Issued by: _____		
Issued On: _____		Signature:

	Witness #2
Expires: _____	Printed Name:

Thumbprint	Thumbprint	Address:
		Phone or Email:
		Signature:

Notary Entry # 55

Date/Time:	_____/_____/_____ _____ am / pm
Location:	
Fee: $_____ Travel: _____	

Type of Service

☐ Acknowledgment   ☐ Jurat
☐ Oath/Affirmation   ☐ Certification
☐ Other: _____   Document Date: _____
Document Type: _____

Individual

Printed Name:	
Address:	

Phone # / Email: _____ _____

Signature:

Identification		Witness #1
☐ Individual	☐ Credible Witness	Printed Name:
☐ Known Personally ☐ Passport		Address:
☐ Driver's License ☐ ID Card		
Other: _____		
ID #: _____		Phone or Email:
Issued by: _____		
Issued On: _____		Signature:
Expires: _____		Witness #2
Thumbprint	Thumbprint	Printed Name:
		Address:
		Phone or Email:
		Signature:

Notary Entry #56

Date/Time:	_____ / _____ / _____ _____ am / pm
Location:	
Fee: $_____ Travel: _____	

Type of Service

☐ Acknowledgment   ☐ Jurat
☐ Oath/Affirmation   ☐ Certification
☐ Other: _____   Document Date: _____
Document Type: _____

Individual Signing

Printed Name:	
Address:	
Phone # / Email: _____ _____	
Signature:	

Identification

☐ Individual   ☐ Credible Witness

☐ Known Personally   ☐ Passport
☐ Driver's License   ☐ ID Card
   Other: _____
ID #: _____
Issued by: _____
Issued On: _____
Expires: _____

Thumbprint	Thumbprint

Witness #1

Printed Name:

Address:

Phone or Email:

Signature:

Witness #2

Printed Name:

Address:

Phone or Email:

Signature:

Notary Entry #57

Date/Time:	_____/_____/_____ _____ am / pm
Location:	
Fee: $_____	Travel: _____

Type of Service

☐ Acknowledgment   ☐ Jurat

☐ Oath/Affirmation   ☐ Certification

☐ Other: _____   Document Date: _____

Document Type: _____

Individual

Printed Name:	
Address:	

Phone # / Email: _____ _____

Signature:

Identification	Witness #1

Identification

☐ Individual   ☐ Credible Witness

☐ Known Personally ☐ Passport

☐ Driver's License   ☐ ID Card

    Other: _____

ID #: _____

Issued by: _____

Issued On: _____

Expires: _____

Witness #1

Printed Name:

Address:

Phone or Email:

Signature:

Witness #2

Printed Name:

Address:

Phone or Email:

Signature:

Thumbprint	Thumbprint

Notary Entry #58

Date/Time:	____/____/_____ ____ am / pm
Location:	
Fee: $_____	Travel: _____

Type of Service

☐ Acknowledgment   ☐ Jurat
☐ Oath/Affirmation   ☐ Certification
☐ Other: _____

Document Date: _____

Document Type: _____

Individual Signing

Printed Name:	
Address:	

Phone # / Email: _____ _____

Signature:

Identification	Witness #1
☐ Individual ☐ Credible Witness	**Printed Name:**
☐ Known Personally ☐ Passport ☐ Driver's License ☐ ID Card Other: _____	Address:
ID #: _____ Issued by: _____	Phone or Email:
Issued On: _____ Expires: _____	Signature:

		Witness #2
Thumbprint	Thumbprint	**Printed Name:**
		Address:
		Phone or Email:
		Signature:

Notary Entry #59

Date/Time:	____/____/_____ ____ am / pm
Location:	
Fee: $_____	Travel: _____

Type of Service

☐ Acknowledgment   ☐ Jurat
☐ Oath/Affirmation   ☐ Certification
☐ Other: _____   Document Date: _____

Document Type: _____

Individual

Printed Name:	
Address:	

Phone # / Email: _____ _____

Signature:

Identification	Witness #1
☐ Individual ☐ Credible Witness	Printed Name:
☐ Known Personally ☐ Passport	Address:
☐ Driver's License ☐ ID Card	
Other: _____	
ID #: _____	Phone or Email:
Issued by: _____	
Issued On: _____	Signature:
Expires: _____	**Witness #2**
Thumbprint Thumbprint	Printed Name:
	Address:
	Phone or Email:
	Signature:

Notary Entry #60

Date/Time:	_____ / _____ / _____ _____ am / pm
Location:	
Fee: $_____ Travel: _____	

Type of Service

☐ Acknowledgment ☐ Jurat

☐ Oath/Affirmation ☐ Certification

☐ Other: _____ Document Date: _____

Document Type: _____

Individual Signing

Printed Name:	
Address:	

Phone # / Email: _____ _____

Signature:

Identification	Witness #1
☐ Individual ☐ Credible Witness	Printed Name:
☐ Known Personally ☐ Passport	Address:
☐ Driver's License ☐ ID Card	
Other: _____	
ID #: _____	Phone or Email:
Issued by: _____	
Issued On: _____	Signature:
Expires: _____	**Witness #2**
	Printed Name:
Thumbprint Thumbprint	Address:
	Phone or Email:
	Signature:

Notary Entry #61

Date/Time:	_____/_____/_____ _____ am / pm
Location:	
Fee: $_____	Travel: _____

Type of Service

☐ Acknowledgment ☐ Jurat
☐ Oath/Affirmation ☐ Certification
☐ Other: _____ Document Date: _____
Document Type: _____

Individual

Printed Name:	
Address:	

Phone # / Email: _____ _____

Signature:

Identification	Witness #1
☐ Individual ☐ Credible Witness	Printed Name:
☐ Known Personally ☐ Passport ☐ Driver's License ☐ ID Card Other: _____	Address:
ID #: _____ Issued by: _____ Issued On: _____ Expires: _____	Phone or Email:
	Signature:
	Witness #2
Thumbprint	Thumbprint	Printed Name:

Thumbprint	Thumbprint	Printed Name:
		Address:
		Phone or Email:
		Signature:

Notary Entry #62

Date/Time:	_____ / _____ / _____ _____ am / pm
Location:	
Fee: $_____ Travel: _____	

Type of Service

☐ Acknowledgment   ☐ Jurat
☐ Oath/Affirmation   ☐ Certification
☐ Other: _____   Document Date: _____
Document Type: _____

Individual Signing

Printed Name:	
Address:	
Phone # / Email: _____ _____	
Signature:	

Identification	Witness #1
☐ Individual ☐ Credible Witness	Printed Name:
☐ Known Personally ☐ Passport ☐ Driver's License ☐ ID Card Other: _____	Address:
ID #: _____ Issued by: _____ Issued On: _____ Expires: _____	Phone or Email:
	Signature:
	Witness #2
Thumbprint Thumbprint	Printed Name:
	Address:
	Phone or Email:
	Signature:

Notary Entry #63

Date/Time:	_____/_____/_____ _____ am / pm
Location:	
Fee: $_____ Travel: _____	

Type of Service

☐ Acknowledgment   ☐ Jurat
☐ Oath/Affirmation   ☐ Certification
☐ Other: _____   Document Date: _____
Document Type: _____

Individual

Printed Name:	
Address:	
Phone # / Email: _____ _____	
Signature:	

Identification	Witness #1
☐ Individual ☐ Credible Witness	Printed Name:
☐ Known Personally ☐ Passport ☐ Driver's License ☐ ID Card	Address:
Other: _____ ID #: _____ Issued by: _____ Issued On: _____	Phone or Email:
Expires: _____	Signature:

		Witness #2
Thumbprint	Thumbprint	Printed Name:
		Address:
		Phone or Email:
		Signature:

Notary Entry #64

Date/Time:	_____/_____/_____ _____ am / pm
Location:	
Fee: $_____ Travel: _____	

Type of Service

☐ Acknowledgment   ☐ Jurat
☐ Oath/Affirmation   ☐ Certification
☐ Other: _____   Document Date: _____
Document Type: _____

Individual Signing

Printed Name:	
Address:	

Phone # / Email: _____ _____

Signature:

Identification	Witness #1
☐ Individual ☐ Credible Witness	Printed Name:
☐ Known Personally ☐ Passport	Address:
☐ Driver's License ☐ ID Card	
Other: _____	
ID #: _____	Phone or Email:
Issued by: _____	
Issued On: _____	Signature:
Expires: _____	**Witness #2**
	Printed Name:
Thumbprint Thumbprint	Address:
	Phone or Email:
	Signature:

Notary Entry # 65

Date/Time:	_____/_____/_____ _____ am / pm
Location:	
Fee: $_____ Travel: _____	

Type of Service

☐ Acknowledgment   ☐ Jurat
☐ Oath/Affirmation   ☐ Certification
☐ Other: _____
Document Date: _____
Document Type: _____

Individual

Printed Name:	
Address:	
Phone # / Email: _____ _____	
Signature:	

Identification	Witness #1
☐ Individual ☐ Credible Witness	Printed Name:
☐ Known Personally ☐ Passport ☐ Driver's License ☐ ID Card Other: _____	Address:
ID #: _____	
Issued by: _____	Phone or Email:
Issued On: _____	
Expires: _____	Signature:
	Witness #2
Thumbprint Thumbprint	Printed Name:
	Address:
	Phone or Email:
	Signature:

Notary Entry #66

Date/Time:	_____/_____/_____ _____ am / pm
Location:	
Fee: $_____	Travel: _____

Type of Service

☐ Acknowledgment   ☐ Jurat
☐ Oath/Affirmation   ☐ Certification
☐ Other: _____   Document Date: _____
Document Type: _____

Individual Signing

Printed Name:	
Address:	

Phone # / Email: _____ _____

Signature:

Identification	Witness #1
☐ Individual ☐ Credible Witness	Printed Name:
☐ Known Personally ☐ Passport	Address:
☐ Driver's License ☐ ID Card	
Other: _____	
ID #: _____	Phone or Email:
Issued by: _____	
Issued On: _____	Signature:
Expires: _____	**Witness #2**
	Printed Name:
Thumbprint	Thumbprint	Address:
		Phone or Email:
		Signature:

Notary Entry # 67

Date/Time:	____ / ____ / _____ ____ am / pm
Location:	
Fee: $_____	Travel: _____

Type of Service

☐ Acknowledgment   ☐ Jurat
☐ Oath/Affirmation   ☐ Certification
☐ Other: _____   Document Date: _____

Document Type: _____

Individual

Printed Name:	
Address:	

Phone # / Email: _____ _____

Signature:

Identification	Witness #1

Identification		Witness #1	
☐ Individual	☐ Credible Witness	Printed Name:	
☐ Known Personally ☐ Passport		Address:	
☐ Driver's License ☐ ID Card			
Other: _____			
ID #: _____		Phone or Email:	
Issued by: _____			
Issued On: _____		Signature:	
Expires: _____		Witness #2	
Thumbprint	Thumbprint	Printed Name:	
		Address:	
		Phone or Email:	
		Signature:	

Notary Entry # 68

Date/Time: _____/_____/_____ _____ am / pm

Location:

Fee: $_____   Travel: _____

Type of Service

☐ Acknowledgment   ☐ Jurat
☐ Oath/Affirmation   ☐ Certification
☐ Other: _____ Document Date: _____
Document Type: _____

Individual Signing

Printed Name:

Address:

Phone # / Email: _____ _____

Signature:

Identification	Witness #1

Identification

☐ Individual   ☐ Credible Witness

☐ Known Personally ☐ Passport
☐ Driver's License ☐ ID Card
   Other: _____
ID #: _____
Issued by: _____
Issued On: _____
Expires: _____

Witness #1

Printed Name:

Address:

Phone or Email:

Signature:

Witness #2

Printed Name:

Address:

Phone or Email:

Signature:

Thumbprint	Thumbprint

Notary Entry #69

Date/Time:	_____/_____/_____ _____ am / pm
Location:	
Fee: $_____ Travel: _____	

Type of Service

☐ Acknowledgment ☐ Jurat
☐ Oath/Affirmation ☐ Certification
☐ Other: _____ Document Date: _____
Document Type: _____

Individual

Printed Name:	
Address:	
Phone # / Email: _____ _____	
Signature:	

Identification	Witness #1
☐ Individual ☐ Credible Witness	Printed Name:
☐ Known Personally ☐ Passport ☐ Driver's License ☐ ID Card Other: _____ ID #: _____ Issued by: _____ Issued On: _____ Expires: _____	Address:
	Phone or Email:
	Signature:
	Witness #2

Thumbprint	Thumbprint	Printed Name:
		Address:
		Phone or Email:
		Signature:

Notary Entry #70

Date/Time:	_____/_____/_____ _____ am / pm
Location:	
Fee: $_____ Travel: _____	

Type of Service

☐ Acknowledgment   ☐ Jurat
☐ Oath/Affirmation   ☐ Certification
☐ Other: _____ Document Date: _____
Document Type: _____

Individual Signing

Printed Name:	
Address:	
Phone # / Email: _____ _____	
Signature:	

Identification		Witness #1
☐ Individual	☐ Credible Witness	Printed Name:
☐ Known Personally ☐ Passport		Address:
☐ Driver's License ☐ ID Card		
Other: _____		
ID #: _____		Phone or Email:
Issued by: _____		
Issued On: _____		Signature:
Expires: _____		**Witness #2**
Thumbprint	Thumbprint	Printed Name:
		Address:
		Phone or Email:
		Signature:

Notary Entry #71

Date/Time:	_____ / _____ / _____ _____ am / pm
Location:	
Fee: $_____ Travel: _____	

Type of Service

☐ Acknowledgment   ☐ Jurat
☐ Oath/Affirmation   ☐ Certification
☐ Other: _____
Document Date: _____
Document Type: _____

Individual

Printed Name:	
Address:	
Phone # / Email: _____ _____	
Signature:	

Identification	Witness #1
☐ Individual ☐ Credible Witness	Printed Name:
☐ Known Personally ☐ Passport	Address:
☐ Driver's License ☐ ID Card	
Other: _____	
ID #: _____	Phone or Email:
Issued by: _____	
Issued On: _____	Signature:
Expires: _____	**Witness #2**
Thumbprint Thumbprint	Printed Name:
	Address:
	Phone or Email:
	Signature:

Notary Entry # 72

Date/Time:	_____/_____/_____ _____ am / pm
Location:	
Fee: $_____	Travel: _____

Type of Service

☐ Acknowledgment   ☐ Jurat
☐ Oath/Affirmation   ☐ Certification
☐ Other: _____   Document Date: _____
Document Type: _____

Individual Signing

Printed Name:	
Address:	

Phone # / Email: _____ _____

Signature:

Identification	Witness #1
☐ Individual ☐ Credible Witness	Printed Name:
☐ Known Personally ☐ Passport	Address:
☐ Driver's License ☐ ID Card	
Other: _____	
ID #: _____	Phone or Email:
Issued by: _____	
Issued On: _____	Signature:
Expires: _____	**Witness #2**
	Printed Name:
Thumbprint Thumbprint	Address:
	Phone or Email:
	Signature:

Notary Entry #73

Date/Time:	_____/_____/_____ _____ am / pm
Location:	
Fee: $_____	Travel: _____

Type of Service

☐ Acknowledgment   ☐ Jurat
☐ Oath/Affirmation   ☐ Certification
☐ Other: _____   Document Date: _____
Document Type: _____

Individual

Printed Name:	
Address:	

Phone # / Email: _____ _____

Signature:

Identification	Witness #1

Identification		Witness #1
☐ Individual ☐ Credible Witness		Printed Name:
☐ Known Personally ☐ Passport		Address:
☐ Driver's License ☐ ID Card		
Other: _____		
ID #: _____		Phone or Email:
Issued by: _____		
Issued On: _____		Signature:
Expires: _____		**Witness #2**
		Printed Name:
Thumbprint	Thumbprint	Address:
		Phone or Email:
		Signature:

Notary Entry #74

Date/Time:	_____/_____/_____ _____ am / pm
Location:	
Fee: $_____ Travel: _____	

Type of Service

☐ Acknowledgment   ☐ Jurat

☐ Oath/Affirmation   ☐ Certification

☐ Other: _____   Document Date: _____

Document Type: _____

Individual Signing

Printed Name:	
Address:	
Phone # / Email: _____ _____	
Signature:	

Identification		Witness #1	
☐ Individual	☐ Credible Witness	Printed Name:	
☐ Known Personally ☐ Passport ☐ Driver's License ☐ ID Card Other: _____		Address:	
ID #: _____ Issued by: _____ Issued On: _____ Expires: _____		Phone or Email:	
		Signature:	
		Witness #2	
Thumbprint	Thumbprint	Printed Name:	
		Address:	
		Phone or Email:	
		Signature:	

Notary Entry #75

Date/Time:	_____/_____/_____ _____ am / pm
Location:	
Fee: $_____	Travel: _____

Type of Service

☐ Acknowledgment   ☐ Jurat
☐ Oath/Affirmation   ☐ Certification
☐ Other: _____ Document Date: _____
Document Type: _____

Individual

Printed Name:	
Address:	

Phone # / Email: _____ _____

Signature:

Identification	Witness #1
☐ Individual ☐ Credible Witness	Printed Name:
☐ Known Personally ☐ Passport	Address:
☐ Driver's License ☐ ID Card	
Other: _____	
ID #: _____	Phone or Email:
Issued by: _____	
Issued On: _____	Signature:
Expires: _____	**Witness #2**
	Printed Name:
Thumbprint Thumbprint	Address:
	Phone or Email:
	Signature:

Notary Entry #76

Date/Time:	_____ / _____ / _____ _____ am / pm
Location:	
Fee: $_____ Travel: _____	

Type of Service

☐ Acknowledgment   ☐ Jurat
☐ Oath/Affirmation   ☐ Certification
☐ Other: _____   Document Date: _____
Document Type: _____

Individual Signing

Printed Name:	
Address:	
Phone # / Email: _____ _____	
Signature:	

Identification		Witness #1	
☐ Individual	☐ Credible Witness	Printed Name:	
☐ Known Personally ☐ Passport		Address:	
☐ Driver's License ☐ ID Card			
Other: _____			
ID #: _____		Phone or Email:	
Issued by: _____			
Issued On: _____		Signature:	
Expires: _____		**Witness #2**	
Thumbprint	Thumbprint	Printed Name:	
		Address:	
		Phone or Email:	
		Signature:	

Notary Entry #77

Date/Time:	_____/_____/_____ _____ am / pm
Location:	
Fee: $_____	Travel: _____

Type of Service

☐ Acknowledgment   ☐ Jurat
☐ Oath/Affirmation   ☐ Certification
☐ Other: _____   Document Date: _____
Document Type: _____

Individual

Printed Name:	
Address:	

Phone # / Email: _____ _____

Signature:

Identification	Witness #1

☐ Individual	☐ Credible Witness	Printed Name:
☐ Known Personally ☐ Passport		Address:
☐ Driver's License ☐ ID Card		
Other: _____		
ID #: _____		Phone or Email:
Issued by: _____		
Issued On: _____		Signature:
Expires: _____		Witness #2

Thumbprint	Thumbprint	Printed Name:
		Address:
		Phone or Email:
		Signature:

Notary Entry #78

Date/Time:	_____/_____/_____ _____ am / pm
Location:	
Fee: $_____ Travel: _____	

Type of Service

☐ Acknowledgment ☐ Jurat
☐ Oath/Affirmation ☐ Certification
☐ Other: _____ Document Date: _____
Document Type: _____

Individual Signing

Printed Name:	
Address:	

Phone # / Email: _____ _____

Signature:

Identification / Witness #1

Identification		Witness #1
☐ Individual	☐ Credible Witness	Printed Name:
☐ Known Personally ☐ Passport		Address:
☐ Driver's License ☐ ID Card		
Other: _____		
ID #: _____		Phone or Email:
Issued by: _____		
Issued On: _____		Signature:
Expires: _____		**Witness #2**
		Printed Name:
Thumbprint	Thumbprint	Address:
		Phone or Email:
		Signature:

Notary Entry #79

Date/Time:	_____/_____/_____ _____ am / pm
Location:	
Fee: $_____ Travel: _____	

Type of Service

☐ Acknowledgment   ☐ Jurat
☐ Oath/Affirmation   ☐ Certification
☐ Other: _____   Document Date: _____
Document Type: _____

Individual

Printed Name:	
Address:	

Phone # / Email: _____ _____

Signature:

Identification		Witness #1	
☐ Individual	☐ Credible Witness	Printed Name:	
☐ Known Personally ☐ Passport		Address:	
☐ Driver's License ☐ ID Card			
Other: _____			
ID #: _____		Phone or Email:	
Issued by: _____			
Issued On: _____		Signature:	
Expires: _____		Witness #2	
Thumbprint	Thumbprint	Printed Name:	
		Address:	
		Phone or Email:	
		Signature:	

Notary Entry #80

Date/Time: _____ / _____ / _____ _____ am / pm

Location:

Fee: $_____ Travel: _____

Type of Service

☐ Acknowledgment   ☐ Jurat
☐ Oath/Affirmation   ☐ Certification
☐ Other: _____   Document Date: _____
Document Type: _____

Individual Signing

Printed Name:

Address:

Phone # / Email: _____ _____

Signature:

Identification	Witness #1
☐ Individual ☐ Credible Witness	Printed Name:
☐ Known Personally ☐ Passport	Address:
☐ Driver's License ☐ ID Card	
Other: _____	
ID #: _____	Phone or Email:
Issued by: _____	
Issued On: _____	Signature:
Expires: _____	Witness #2
Thumbprint Thumbprint	Printed Name:
	Address:
	Phone or Email:
	Signature:

Notary Entry #81

Date/Time:	_____/_____/_____ _____ am / pm
Location:	
Fee: $_____ Travel: _____	

Type of Service

☐ Acknowledgment   ☐ Jurat
☐ Oath/Affirmation   ☐ Certification
☐ Other: _____   Document Date: _____
Document Type: _____

Individual

Printed Name:	
Address:	
Phone # / Email: _____ _____	
Signature:	

Identification		Witness #1	
☐ Individual	☐ Credible Witness	Printed Name:	
☐ Known Personally ☐ Passport ☐ Driver's License ☐ ID Card Other: _____ ID #: _____ Issued by: _____ Issued On: _____ Expires: _____		Address:	
		Phone or Email:	
		Signature:	
		Witness #2	
Thumbprint	Thumbprint	Printed Name:	
		Address:	
		Phone or Email:	
		Signature:	

Notary Entry # 82

Date/Time:	_____/_____/_____ _____ am / pm
Location:	
Fee: $_____	Travel: _____

Type of Service

☐ Acknowledgment ☐ Jurat
☐ Oath/Affirmation ☐ Certification
☐ Other: _____ Document Date: _____
Document Type: _____

Individual Signing

Printed Name:	
Address:	
Phone # / Email:	_____ _____
Signature:	

Identification	Witness #1
☐ Individual ☐ Credible Witness	Printed Name:
☐ Known Personally ☐ Passport ☐ Driver's License ☐ ID Card Other: _____ ID #: _____ Issued by: _____ Issued On: _____ Expires: _____	Address:
	Phone or Email:
	Signature:
	Witness #2
Thumbprint	Printed Name:
	Address:
Thumbprint	Phone or Email:
	Signature:

Notary Entry #83

Date/Time:	_____ / _____ / _____ _____ am / pm
Location:	
Fee: $_____ Travel: _____	

Type of Service

☐ Acknowledgment   ☐ Jurat
☐ Oath/Affirmation   ☐ Certification
☐ Other: _____   Document Date: _____
Document Type: _____

Individual

Printed Name:	
Address:	

Phone # / Email: _____ _____

Signature:

Identification	Witness #1

☐ Individual	☐ Credible Witness	Printed Name:
☐ Known Personally ☐ Passport		Address:
☐ Driver's License ☐ ID Card		
Other: _____		
ID #: _____		Phone or Email:
Issued by: _____		
Issued On: _____		Signature:
Expires: _____		**Witness #2**
Thumbprint	Thumbprint	Printed Name:
		Address:
		Phone or Email:
		Signature:

Notary Entry # 84

Date/Time: _____ / _____ / _____ _____ am / pm

Location:

Fee: $_____ Travel: _____

Type of Service

☐ Acknowledgment   ☐ Jurat
☐ Oath/Affirmation   ☐ Certification
☐ Other: _____   Document Date: _____
Document Type: _____

Individual Signing

Printed Name:

Address:

Phone # / Email: _____ _____

Signature:

Identification	Witness #1

Identification

☐ Individual   ☐ Credible Witness
☐ Known Personally ☐ Passport
☐ Driver's License ☐ ID Card
    Other: _____
ID #: _____
Issued by: _____
Issued On: _____
Expires: _____

Witness #1

Printed Name:
Address:

Phone or Email:
Signature:

Witness #2

Printed Name:
Address:

Phone or Email:
Signature:

Thumbprint	Thumbprint

Notary Entry #85

Date/Time: _____/_____/_____ _____ am / pm

Location:

Fee: $_____   Travel: _____

Type of Service

☐ Acknowledgment   ☐ Jurat
☐ Oath/Affirmation   ☐ Certification
☐ Other: _____   Document Date: _____
Document Type: _____

Individual

Printed Name:

Address:

Phone # / Email: _____ _____

Signature:

Identification	Witness #1

Identification

☐ Individual   ☐ Credible Witness

☐ Known Personally ☐ Passport
☐ Driver's License ☐ ID Card
  Other: _____
ID #: _____
Issued by: _____
Issued On: _____
Expires: _____

Thumbprint	Thumbprint

Witness #1

Printed Name:

Address:

Phone or Email:

Signature:

Witness #2

Printed Name:

Address:

Phone or Email:

Signature:

Notary Entry #86

Date/Time:	_____/_____/_____ _____ am / pm
Location:	
Fee: $_____	Travel: _____

Type of Service

☐ Acknowledgment   ☐ Jurat

☐ Oath/Affirmation   ☐ Certification

☐ Other: _____   Document Date: _____

Document Type: _____

Individual Signing

Printed Name:	
Address:	
Phone # / Email: _____ _____	
Signature:	

Identification

☐ Individual   ☐ Credible Witness

☐ Known Personally   ☐ Passport

☐ Driver's License   ☐ ID Card

    Other: _____

ID #: _____

Issued by: _____

Issued On: _____

Expires: _____

Thumbprint	Thumbprint

Witness #1

Printed Name:

Address:

Phone or Email:

Signature:

Witness #2

Printed Name:

Address:

Phone or Email:

Signature:

Notary Entry #87

Date/Time:	____/____/_____ ____ am / pm
Location:	
Fee: $_____	Travel: _____

Type of Service

☐ Acknowledgment   ☐ Jurat

☐ Oath/Affirmation   ☐ Certification

☐ Other: _____   Document Date: _____

Document Type: _____

Individual

Printed Name:	
Address:	
Phone # / Email: _____ _____
Signature:

Identification	Witness #1

Identification

☐ Individual   ☐ Credible Witness

☐ Known Personally ☐ Passport

☐ Driver's License ☐ ID Card

   Other: _____

ID #: _____

Issued by: _____

Issued On: _____

Expires: _____

Witness #1

Printed Name:

Address:

Phone or Email:

Signature:

Witness #2

Printed Name:

Address:

Phone or Email:

Signature:

Thumbprint	Thumbprint

Notary Entry #88

Date/Time:	_____ / _____ / _____ _____ am / pm
Location:	
Fee: $_____ Travel: _____	

Type of Service

☐ Acknowledgment   ☐ Jurat
☐ Oath/Affirmation   ☐ Certification
☐ Other: _____   Document Date: _____
Document Type: _____

Individual Signing

Printed Name:	
Address:	
Phone # / Email: _____ _____	
Signature:	

Identification		Witness #1

☐ Individual	☐ Credible Witness	Printed Name:
☐ Known Personally ☐ Passport		Address:
☐ Driver's License ☐ ID Card		
Other: _____		
ID #: _____		Phone or Email:
Issued by: _____		
Issued On: _____		Signature:
Expires: _____		**Witness #2**
Thumbprint	Thumbprint	Printed Name:
		Address:
		Phone or Email:
		Signature:

Notary Entry # 89

Date/Time:	_____/_____/_____ _____ am / pm
Location:	
Fee: $_____ Travel: _____	

Type of Service

☐ Acknowledgment   ☐ Jurat
☐ Oath/Affirmation   ☐ Certification
☐ Other: _____   Document Date: _____
Document Type: _____

Individual

Printed Name:	
Address:	

Phone # / Email: _____ _____

Signature:

Identification	Witness #1
☐ Individual ☐ Credible Witness	Printed Name:
☐ Known Personally ☐ Passport	Address:
☐ Driver's License ☐ ID Card	
Other: _____	
ID #: _____	Phone or Email:
Issued by: _____	
Issued On: _____	Signature:
Expires: _____	Witness #2
	Printed Name:
Thumbprint Thumbprint	Address:
	Phone or Email:
	Signature:

Notary Entry #90

Date/Time:	____/____/_____ ____ am / pm
Location:	
Fee: $_____	Travel: _____

Type of Service

☐ Acknowledgment   ☐ Jurat
☐ Oath/Affirmation   ☐ Certification
☐ Other: _____   Document Date: _____

Document Type: _____

Individual Signing

Printed Name:	
Address:	
Phone # / Email:	_____ _____
Signature:	

Identification	Witness #1

Identification		Witness #1
☐ Individual	☐ Credible Witness	Printed Name:
☐ Known Personally ☐ Passport		Address:
☐ Driver's License ☐ ID Card		
Other: _____		
ID #: _____		Phone or Email:
Issued by: _____		
Issued On: _____		Signature:
Expires: _____		**Witness #2**

Thumbprint	Thumbprint	Printed Name:
		Address:
		Phone or Email:
		Signature:

Notary Entry #91

Date/Time:	____/____/_____ ____ am / pm
Location:	
Fee: $_____ Travel: _____	

Type of Service

☐ Acknowledgment   ☐ Jurat
☐ Oath/Affirmation   ☐ Certification
☐ Other: _____   Document Date: _____
Document Type: _____

Individual

Printed Name:	
Address:	
Phone # / Email: _____ _____	
Signature:	

Identification	Witness #1
☐ Individual ☐ Credible Witness	Printed Name:
☐ Known Personally ☐ Passport ☐ Driver's License ☐ ID Card Other: _____ ID #: _____ Issued by: _____ Issued On: _____ Expires: _____	Address:
	Phone or Email:
	Signature:
	Witness #2
Thumbprint	Thumbprint	Printed Name:

Thumbprint	Thumbprint	Address:
		Phone or Email:
		Signature:

Notary Entry # 92

Date/Time:	_____ / _____ / _____ _____ am / pm
Location:	
Fee: $_____ Travel: _____	

Type of Service

☐ Acknowledgment   ☐ Jurat
☐ Oath/Affirmation   ☐ Certification
☐ Other: _____   Document Date: _____
Document Type: _____

Individual Signing

Printed Name:	
Address:	

Phone # / Email: _____ _____

Signature:

Identification / Witness #1

Identification

☐ Individual   ☐ Credible Witness
☐ Known Personally   ☐ Passport
☐ Driver's License   ☐ ID Card
    Other: _____
ID #: _____
Issued by: _____
Issued On: _____
Expires: _____

Witness #1

Printed Name:

Address:

Phone or Email:

Signature:

Thumbprint	Thumbprint

Witness #2

Printed Name:

Address:

Phone or Email:

Signature:

Notary Entry #93

Date/Time:	_____/_____/_____ _____ am / pm
Location:	
Fee: $_____ Travel: _____	

Type of Service

☐ Acknowledgment   ☐ Jurat
☐ Oath/Affirmation   ☐ Certification
☐ Other: _____   Document Date: _____
Document Type: _____

Individual

Printed Name:	
Address:	
Phone # / Email: _____ _____	
Signature:	

Identification	Witness #1
☐ Individual ☐ Credible Witness	Printed Name:
☐ Known Personally ☐ Passport ☐ Driver's License ☐ ID Card Other: _____	Address:
ID #: _____	Phone or Email:
Issued by: _____	
Issued On: _____	Signature:
Expires: _____	**Witness #2**
Thumbprint Thumbprint	Printed Name:
	Address:
	Phone or Email:
	Signature:

Notary Entry # 94

Date/Time:	_____/_____/_____ _____ am / pm
Location:	
Fee: $_____	Travel: _____

Type of Service

☐ Acknowledgment   ☐ Jurat
☐ Oath/Affirmation   ☐ Certification
☐ Other: _____
Document Date: _____
Document Type: _____

Individual Signing

Printed Name:	
Address:	
Phone # / Email:	_____ _____
Signature:	

Identification

☐ Individual   ☐ Credible Witness
☐ Known Personally   ☐ Passport
☐ Driver's License   ☐ ID Card
     Other: _____
ID #: _____
Issued by: _____
Issued On: _____
Expires: _____

Thumbprint	Thumbprint

Witness #1

Printed Name:
Address:

Phone or Email:
Signature:

Witness #2

Printed Name:
Address:

Phone or Email:
Signature:

Notary Entry #95

Date/Time:	_____/_____/_____ _____ am / pm
Location:	
Fee: $_____	Travel: _____

Type of Service

☐ Acknowledgment   ☐ Jurat
☐ Oath/Affirmation   ☐ Certification
☐ Other: _____   Document Date: _____
Document Type: _____

Individual

Printed Name:	
Address:	

Phone # / Email: _____ _____

Signature:

Identification	Witness #1

Identification		Witness #1
☐ Individual	☐ Credible Witness	Printed Name:
☐ Known Personally ☐ Passport		Address:
☐ Driver's License ☐ ID Card		
Other: _____		
ID #: _____		Phone or Email:
Issued by: _____		
Issued On: _____		Signature:
Expires: _____		**Witness #2**

Thumbprint	Thumbprint	Printed Name:
		Address:
		Phone or Email:
		Signature:

Notary Entry #96

Date/Time:	_____/_____/_____ _____ am / pm
Location:	
Fee: $_____	Travel: _____

Type of Service

☐ Acknowledgment   ☐ Jurat

☐ Oath/Affirmation   ☐ Certification

☐ Other: _____   Document Date: _____

Document Type: _____

Individual Signing

Printed Name:	
Address:	

Phone # / Email: _____ _____

Signature:

Identification	Witness #1

Identification		Witness #1	
☐ Individual	☐ Credible Witness	Printed Name:	
☐ Known Personally	☐ Passport	Address:	
☐ Driver's License	☐ ID Card		
Other: _____		Phone or Email:	
ID #: _____			
Issued by: _____			
Issued On: _____		Signature:	
Expires: _____		Witness #2	
Thumbprint	Thumbprint	Printed Name:	
		Address:	
		Phone or Email:	
		Signature:	

Notary Entry #97

Date/Time:	_____/_____/_____ _____ am / pm
Location:	
Fee: $_____	Travel: _____

Type of Service

☐ Acknowledgment   ☐ Jurat
☐ Oath/Affirmation   ☐ Certification
☐ Other: _____   Document Date: _____
Document Type: _____

Individual

Printed Name:	
Address:	

Phone # / Email: _____ _____

Signature:

Identification	Witness #1

☐ Individual	☐ Credible Witness	Printed Name:
☐ Known Personally ☐ Passport ☐ Driver's License ☐ ID Card Other: _____		Address:
ID #: _____ Issued by: _____ Issued On: _____		Phone or Email:
Expires: _____		Signature:

Witness #2

Thumbprint	Thumbprint	Printed Name:
		Address:
		Phone or Email:
		Signature:

Notary Entry #98

Date/Time:	_____/_____/_____ _____ am / pm
Location:	
Fee: $_____	Travel: _____

Type of Service

☐ Acknowledgment   ☐ Jurat
☐ Oath/Affirmation   ☐ Certification
☐ Other: _____   Document Date: _____

Document Type: _____

Individual Signing

Printed Name:	
Address:	

Phone # / Email: _____ _____

Signature:

Identification	Witness #1

Identification

☐ Individual   ☐ Credible Witness
☐ Known Personally   ☐ Passport
☐ Driver's License   ☐ ID Card
    Other: _____
ID #: _____
Issued by: _____
Issued On: _____
Expires: _____

Witness #1

Printed Name:

Address:

Phone or Email:

Signature:

Witness #2

Printed Name:

Address:

Phone or Email:

Signature:

Thumbprint	Thumbprint

Notary Entry #99

Date/Time:	_____ / _____ / _____ _____ am / pm
Location:	
Fee: $_____ Travel: _____	

Type of Service

☐ Acknowledgment　　☐ Jurat
☐ Oath/Affirmation　　☐ Certification
☐ Other: _____　Document Date: _____
Document Type: _____

Individual

Printed Name:	
Address:	

Phone # / Email: _____ _____

Signature:

Identification		Witness #1
☐ Individual	☐ Credible Witness	Printed Name:
☐ Known Personally ☐ Passport		Address:
☐ Driver's License ☐ ID Card		
Other: _____		
ID #: _____		Phone or Email:
Issued by: _____		
Issued On: _____		Signature:
Expires: _____		**Witness #2**
Thumbprint	Thumbprint	Printed Name:
		Address:
		Phone or Email:
		Signature:

Notary Entry #100

Date/Time:	_____ / _____ / _____ _____ am / pm
Location:	
Fee: $_____ Travel: _____	

Type of Service

☐ Acknowledgment   ☐ Jurat
☐ Oath/Affirmation   ☐ Certification
☐ Other: _____

Document Date: _____

Document Type: _____

Individual Signing

Printed Name:	
Address:	
Phone # / Email: _____ _____	
Signature:	

Identification	Witness #1

☐ Individual	☐ Credible Witness	Printed Name:
☐ Known Personally ☐ Passport ☐ Driver's License ☐ ID Card		Address:
Other: _____		
ID #: _____ Issued by: _____		Phone or Email:
Issued On: _____ Expires: _____		Signature:

		Witness #2
Thumbprint	Thumbprint	Printed Name:
		Address:
		Phone or Email:
		Signature:

Notary Entry #101

Date/Time:	_____/_____/_____ _____ am / pm
Location:	
Fee: $_____ Travel: _____	

Type of Service

☐ Acknowledgment   ☐ Jurat
☐ Oath/Affirmation   ☐ Certification
☐ Other: _____ Document Date: _____
Document Type: _____

Individual

Printed Name:	
Address:	
Phone # / Email: _____ _____	
Signature:	

Identification	Witness #1
☐ Individual ☐ Credible Witness	Printed Name:
☐ Known Personally ☐ Passport ☐ Driver's License ☐ ID Card Other: _____ ID #: _____ Issued by: _____ Issued On: _____	Address:
	Phone or Email:
Expires: _____	Signature:
	Witness #2
Thumbprint Thumbprint	Printed Name:
	Address:
	Phone or Email:
	Signature:

Notary Entry #102

Date/Time:	_____ / _____ / _____ _____ am / pm
Location:	
Fee: $_____ Travel: _____	

Type of Service

☐ Acknowledgment   ☐ Jurat
☐ Oath/Affirmation   ☐ Certification
☐ Other: _____ Document Date: _____
Document Type: _____

Individual Signing

Printed Name:	
Address:	

Phone # / Email: _____ _____

Signature:

Identification	Witness #1
☐ Individual ☐ Credible Witness	Printed Name:
☐ Known Personally ☐ Passport	Address:
☐ Driver's License ☐ ID Card	
Other: _____	
ID #: _____	Phone or Email:
Issued by: _____	
Issued On: _____	Signature:
Expires: _____	**Witness #2**
	Printed Name:
Thumbprint	Thumbprint	Address:
		Phone or Email:
		Signature:

Notary Entry #103

Date/Time:	_____/_____/_____ _____ am / pm
Location:	
Fee: $_____ Travel: _____	

Type of Service

☐ Acknowledgment   ☐ Jurat
☐ Oath/Affirmation   ☐ Certification
☐ Other: _____   Document Date: _____
Document Type: _____

Individual

Printed Name:	
Address:	

Phone # / Email: _____ _____

Signature:

Identification	Witness #1
☐ Individual ☐ Credible Witness	Printed Name:
☐ Known Personally ☐ Passport ☐ Driver's License ☐ ID Card	Address:
Other: _____	
ID #: _____	Phone or Email:
Issued by: _____	
Issued On: _____	Signature:
Expires: _____	**Witness #2**
	Printed Name:
Thumbprint Thumbprint	Address:
	Phone or Email:
	Signature:

Notary Entry #104

Date/Time:	_____/_____/_____ ____ am / pm
Location:	
Fee: $_____	Travel: _____

Type of Service

☐ Acknowledgment   ☐ Jurat
☐ Oath/Affirmation   ☐ Certification
☐ Other: _____

Document Date: _____

Document Type: _____

Individual Signing

Printed Name:	
Address:	
Phone # / Email:	_____ _____
Signature:	

Identification	Witness #1

Identification

☐ Individual   ☐ Credible Witness
☐ Known Personally   ☐ Passport
☐ Driver's License   ☐ ID Card
Other: _____
ID #: _____
Issued by: _____
Issued On: _____
Expires: _____

Witness #1

Printed Name:
Address:

Phone or Email:
Signature:

Witness #2

Printed Name:
Address:

Phone or Email:
Signature:

Thumbprint	Thumbprint

Notary Entry #105

Date/Time:	_____ / _____ / _____ _____ am / pm
Location:	
Fee: $_____ Travel: _____	

Type of Service

☐ Acknowledgment   ☐ Jurat
☐ Oath/Affirmation   ☐ Certification
☐ Other: _____   Document Date: _____
Document Type: _____

Individual

Printed Name:	
Address:	

Phone # / Email: _____ _____

Signature:

Identification	Witness #1
☐ Individual ☐ Credible Witness	Printed Name:
☐ Known Personally ☐ Passport	Address:
☐ Driver's License ☐ ID Card	
Other: _____	
ID #: _____	Phone or Email:
Issued by: _____	
Issued On: _____	Signature:
Expires: _____	**Witness #2**
	Printed Name:
Thumbprint Thumbprint	Address:
	Phone or Email:
	Signature:

Notary Entry #106

Date/Time:	_____ / _____ / _____ _____ am / pm
Location:	
Fee: $_____ Travel: _____	

Type of Service

☐ Acknowledgment   ☐ Jurat
☐ Oath/Affirmation   ☐ Certification
☐ Other: _____   Document Date: _____
Document Type: _____

Individual Signing

Printed Name:	
Address:	
Phone # / Email: _____ _____	
Signature:	

Identification	Witness #1
☐ Individual ☐ Credible Witness	Printed Name:
☐ Known Personally ☐ Passport ☐ Driver's License ☐ ID Card	Address:
Other: _____	
ID #: _____	Phone or Email:
Issued by: _____	
Issued On: _____	Signature:
Expires: _____	**Witness #2**
	Printed Name:
Thumbprint Thumbprint	Address:
	Phone or Email:
	Signature:

Notary Entry #107

Date/Time:	____/____/_____ ____ am / pm
Location:	
Fee: $_____ Travel: _____	

Type of Service

☐ Acknowledgment   ☐ Jurat
☐ Oath/Affirmation   ☐ Certification
☐ Other: _____   Document Date: _____
Document Type: _____

Individual

Printed Name:	
Address:	

Phone # / Email: _____ _____

Signature:

Identification	Witness #1
☐ Individual ☐ Credible Witness	Printed Name:
☐ Known Personally ☐ Passport ☐ Driver's License ☐ ID Card	Address:
Other: _____	
ID #: _____	Phone or Email:
Issued by: _____	
Issued On: _____	Signature:
Expires: _____	Witness #2

Thumbprint	Thumbprint	Printed Name:
		Address:
		Phone or Email:
		Signature:

Notary Entry #108

Date/Time:	____ / ____ / _____ ____ am / pm
Location:	
Fee: $_____	Travel: _____

Type of Service

☐ Acknowledgment   ☐ Jurat
☐ Oath/Affirmation   ☐ Certification
☐ Other: _____

Document Date: _____

Document Type: _____

Individual Signing

Printed Name:	
Address:	
Phone # / Email:	_____ _____
Signature:	

Identification	Witness #1

Identification

☐ Individual   ☐ Credible Witness
☐ Known Personally   ☐ Passport
☐ Driver's License   ☐ ID Card
   Other: _____
ID #: _____
Issued by: _____
Issued On: _____
Expires: _____

Witness #1

Printed Name:
Address:

Phone or Email:
Signature:

Thumbprint	Thumbprint

Witness #2

Printed Name:
Address:

Phone or Email:
Signature:

Notary Entry #109

Date/Time:	___/___/_____ ____ am / pm
Location:	
Fee: $_____	Travel: _____

Type of Service

☐ Acknowledgment   ☐ Jurat
☐ Oath/Affirmation   ☐ Certification
☐ Other: _____ Document Date: _____
Document Type: _____

Individual

Printed Name:	
Address:	

Phone # / Email: _____ _____

Signature:

Identification	Witness #1
☐ Individual ☐ Credible Witness	Printed Name:
☐ Known Personally ☐ Passport ☐ Driver's License ☐ ID Card	Address:
Other: _____	
ID #: _____	Phone or Email:
Issued by: _____	
Issued On: _____	Signature:
Expires: _____	Witness #2
Thumbprint Thumbprint	Printed Name:
	Address:
	Phone or Email:
	Signature:

Notary Entry #110

Date/Time:	_____/_____/_____ _____ am / pm
Location:	
Fee: $_____ Travel: _____	

Type of Service

☐ Acknowledgment   ☐ Jurat

☐ Oath/Affirmation   ☐ Certification

☐ Other: _____   Document Date: _____

Document Type: _____

Individual Signing

Printed Name:	
Address:	
Phone # / Email: _____ _____	
Signature:	

Identification		Witness #1
☐ Individual	☐ Credible Witness	Printed Name:
☐ Known Personally ☐ Passport		Address:
☐ Driver's License ☐ ID Card		
Other: _____		
ID #: _____		Phone or Email:
Issued by: _____		
Issued On: _____		Signature:
Expires: _____		Witness #2
Thumbprint	Thumbprint	Printed Name:
		Address:
		Phone or Email:
		Signature:

Notary Entry #111

Date/Time:	_____/_____/_____ _____ am / pm
Location:	
Fee: $_____	Travel: _____

Type of Service

☐ Acknowledgment   ☐ Jurat

☐ Oath/Affirmation   ☐ Certification

☐ Other: _____   Document Date: _____

Document Type: _____

Individual

Printed Name:	
Address:	

Phone # / Email: _____ _____

Signature:

Identification	Witness #1
☐ Individual ☐ Credible Witness	Printed Name:
☐ Known Personally ☐ Passport	Address:
☐ Driver's License ☐ ID Card	
Other: _____	
ID #: _____	Phone or Email:
Issued by: _____	
Issued On: _____	Signature:
Expires: _____	**Witness #2**
	Printed Name:
Thumbprint Thumbprint	Address:
	Phone or Email:
	Signature:

Notary Entry #112

Date/Time: _____/_____/_____ _____ am / pm

Location:

Fee: $_____   Travel: _____

Type of Service

☐ Acknowledgment   ☐ Jurat
☐ Oath/Affirmation   ☐ Certification
☐ Other: _____   Document Date: _____
Document Type: _____

Individual Signing

Printed Name:

Address:

Phone # / Email: _____ _____

Signature:

Identification		Witness #1

Identification

☐ Individual   ☐ Credible Witness

☐ Known Personally ☐ Passport
☐ Driver's License ☐ ID Card
    Other: _____
ID #: _____
Issued by: _____
Issued On: _____
Expires: _____

Witness #1

Printed Name:
Address:

Phone or Email:

Signature:

Witness #2

Printed Name:
Address:

Phone or Email:

Signature:

Thumbprint	Thumbprint

Notary Entry #113

Date/Time:	____/____/_____ ____ am / pm
Location:	
Fee: $_____ Travel: _____	

Type of Service

☐ Acknowledgment   ☐ Jurat
☐ Oath/Affirmation   ☐ Certification
☐ Other: _____   Document Date: _____
Document Type: _____

Individual

Printed Name:	
Address:	
Phone # / Email: _____ _____	
Signature:	

Identification	Witness #1
☐ Individual ☐ Credible Witness	Printed Name:
☐ Known Personally ☐ Passport ☐ Driver's License ☐ ID Card Other: _____ ID #: _____ Issued by: _____ Issued On: _____ Expires: _____	Address:
	Phone or Email:
	Signature:
	Witness #2
Thumbprint Thumbprint	Printed Name:
	Address:
	Phone or Email:
	Signature:

Notary Entry #114

Date/Time:	_____/_____/_____ _____ am / pm
Location:	
Fee: $_____ Travel: _____	

Type of Service

☐ Acknowledgment ☐ Jurat
☐ Oath/Affirmation ☐ Certification
☐ Other: _____ Document Date: _____
Document Type: _____

Individual Signing

Printed Name:	
Address:	
Phone # / Email: _____ _____	
Signature:	

Identification	Witness #1
☐ Individual ☐ Credible Witness	Printed Name:
☐ Known Personally ☐ Passport ☐ Driver's License ☐ ID Card Other: _____ ID #: _____ Issued by: _____ Issued On: _____ Expires: _____	Address:
	Phone or Email:
	Signature:
	Witness #2
Thumbprint Thumbprint	Printed Name:
	Address:
	Phone or Email:
	Signature:

Notary Entry #115

Date/Time:	_____/_____/_____ ____ am / pm
Location:	

Fee: $_____   Travel: _____

Type of Service

☐ Acknowledgment ☐ Jurat
☐ Oath/Affirmation ☐ Certification
☐ Other: _____   Document Date: _____
Document Type: _____

Individual

Printed Name:	
Address:	

Phone # / Email: _____ _____

Signature:

Identification	Witness #1
☐ Individual ☐ Credible Witness	Printed Name:
☐ Known Personally ☐ Passport ☐ Driver's License ☐ ID Card Other: _____ ID #: _____ Issued by: _____ Issued On: _____ Expires: _____	Address:
	Phone or Email:
	Signature:
	Witness #2
Thumbprint Thumbprint	Printed Name:
	Address:
	Phone or Email:
	Signature:

Notary Entry #116

Date/Time:	_____/_____/_____ _____ am / pm
Location:	
Fee: $_____ Travel: _____	

Type of Service

☐ Acknowledgment ☐ Jurat
☐ Oath/Affirmation ☐ Certification
☐ Other: _____ Document Date: _____
Document Type: _____

Individual Signing

Printed Name:	
Address:	

Phone # / Email: _____ _____

Signature:

Identification	Witness #1
☐ Individual ☐ Credible Witness	Printed Name:
☐ Known Personally ☐ Passport	Address:
☐ Driver's License ☐ ID Card	
Other: _____	
ID #: _____	Phone or Email:
Issued by: _____	
Issued On: _____	Signature:
Expires: _____	Witness #2
Thumbprint	Thumbprint	Printed Name:
		Address:
		Phone or Email:
		Signature:

Notary Entry #117

Date/Time:	_____/_____/_____ _____ am / pm
Location:	
Fee: $_____ Travel: _____	

Type of Service

☐ Acknowledgment   ☐ Jurat
☐ Oath/Affirmation   ☐ Certification
☐ Other: _____   Document Date: _____
Document Type: _____

Individual

Printed Name:	
Address:	

Phone # / Email: _____ _____

Signature:

Identification	Witness #1
☐ Individual ☐ Credible Witness	Printed Name:
☐ Known Personally ☐ Passport ☐ Driver's License ☐ ID Card	Address:
Other: _____	
ID #: _____	Phone or Email:
Issued by: _____	
Issued On: _____	Signature:
Expires: _____	**Witness #2**

Thumbprint	Thumbprint	Printed Name:
		Address:
		Phone or Email:
		Signature:

Notary Entry #118

Date/Time:	_____/_____/_____ _____ am / pm
Location:	
Fee: $_____ Travel: _____	

Type of Service

☐ Acknowledgment   ☐ Jurat
☐ Oath/Affirmation   ☐ Certification
☐ Other: _____   Document Date: _____
Document Type: _____

Individual Signing

Printed Name:	
Address:	
Phone # / Email: _____ _____	
Signature:	

Identification		Witness #1
☐ Individual	☐ Credible Witness	Printed Name:
☐ Known Personally ☐ Passport		Address:
☐ Driver's License ☐ ID Card		
Other: _____		
ID #: _____		Phone or Email:
Issued by: _____		
Issued On: _____		Signature:
Expires: _____		**Witness #2**
Thumbprint	Thumbprint	Printed Name:
		Address:
		Phone or Email:
		Signature:

Notary Entry #119

Date/Time:	_____ / _____ / _____ _____ am / pm
Location:	
Fee: $_____ Travel: _____	

Type of Service

☐ Acknowledgment   ☐ Jurat
☐ Oath/Affirmation   ☐ Certification
☐ Other: _____   Document Date: _____
Document Type: _____

Individual

Printed Name:	
Address:	

Phone # / Email: _____ _____

Signature:

Identification	Witness #1
☐ Individual ☐ Credible Witness	Printed Name:
☐ Known Personally ☐ Passport ☐ Driver's License ☐ ID Card Other: _____ ID #: _____ Issued by: _____ Issued On: _____ Expires: _____	Address: Phone or Email: Signature:
	Witness #2
Thumbprint Thumbprint	Printed Name:
	Address: Phone or Email: Signature:

Notary Entry #120

Date/Time:	_____/_____/_____ _____ am / pm
Location:	
Fee: $_____ Travel: _____	

Type of Service

☐ Acknowledgment   ☐ Jurat
☐ Oath/Affirmation   ☐ Certification
☐ Other: _____   Document Date: _____
Document Type: _____

Individual Signing

Printed Name:	
Address:	

Phone # / Email: _____ _____

Signature:

Identification	Witness #1

☐ Individual	☐ Credible Witness	Printed Name:
☐ Known Personally ☐ Passport		Address:
☐ Driver's License ☐ ID Card		
Other: _____		
ID #: _____		Phone or Email:
Issued by: _____		
Issued On: _____		Signature:
Expires: _____		**Witness #2**

Thumbprint	Thumbprint	Printed Name:
		Address:
		Phone or Email:
		Signature:

Notary Entry #121

Date/Time:	_____/_____/_____ _____ am / pm
Location:	
Fee: $_____ Travel: _____	

Type of Service

☐ Acknowledgment   ☐ Jurat
☐ Oath/Affirmation   ☐ Certification
☐ Other: _____   Document Date: _____
Document Type: _____

Individual

Printed Name:	
Address:	

Phone # / Email: _____ _____

Signature:

Identification	Witness #1
☐ Individual ☐ Credible Witness	Printed Name:
☐ Known Personally ☐ Passport ☐ Driver's License ☐ ID Card Other: _____ ID #: _____ Issued by: _____ Issued On: _____ Expires: _____	Address:
	Phone or Email:
	Signature:
	Witness #2
Thumbprint Thumbprint	Printed Name:
	Address:
	Phone or Email:
	Signature:

Notary Entry #122

Date/Time:	_____/_____/_____ _____ am / pm
Location:	
Fee: $_____	Travel: _____

Type of Service

☐ Acknowledgment   ☐ Jurat

☐ Oath/Affirmation   ☐ Certification

☐ Other: _____   Document Date: _____

Document Type: _____

Individual Signing

Printed Name:	
Address:	
Phone # / Email: _____ _____	
Signature:	

Identification	Witness #1
☐ Individual ☐ Credible Witness	Printed Name:
☐ Known Personally ☐ Passport ☐ Driver's License ☐ ID Card	Address:
Other: _____	
ID #: _____	Phone or Email:
Issued by: _____	
Issued On: _____	Signature:
Expires: _____	**Witness #2**

		Witness #2
Thumbprint	Thumbprint	Printed Name:
		Address:
		Phone or Email:
		Signature:

Notary Entry #123

Date/Time:	_____ / _____ / _____ _____ am / pm
Location:	
Fee: $_____ Travel: _____	

Type of Service

☐ Acknowledgment   ☐ Jurat
☐ Oath/Affirmation   ☐ Certification
☐ Other: _____   Document Date: _____
Document Type: _____

Individual

Printed Name:	
Address:	
Phone # / Email: _____ _____	
Signature:	

Identification		Witness #1
☐ Individual	☐ Credible Witness	Printed Name:
☐ Known Personally ☐ Passport		Address:
☐ Driver's License ☐ ID Card		
Other: _____		
ID #: _____		Phone or Email:
Issued by: _____		
Issued On: _____		Signature:
Expires: _____		**Witness #2**
Thumbprint	Thumbprint	Printed Name:
		Address:
		Phone or Email:
		Signature:

Notary Entry #124

Date/Time:	_____ / _____ / _____ _____ am / pm
Location:	
Fee: $_____ Travel: _____	

Type of Service

☐ Acknowledgment   ☐ Jurat
☐ Oath/Affirmation   ☐ Certification
☐ Other: _____   Document Date: _____
Document Type: _____

Individual Signing

Printed Name:	
Address:	
Phone # / Email: _____ _____	
Signature:	

Identification		Witness #1
☐ Individual	☐ Credible Witness	Printed Name:
☐ Known Personally ☐ Passport		Address:
☐ Driver's License ☐ ID Card		
Other: _____		
ID #: _____		Phone or Email:
Issued by: _____		
Issued On: _____		Signature:
Expires: _____		Witness #2
Thumbprint	Thumbprint	Printed Name:
		Address:
		Phone or Email:
		Signature:

Notary Entry #125

Date/Time:	_____/_____/_____ _____ am / pm
Location:	
Fee: $_____ Travel: _____	

Type of Service

☐ Acknowledgment   ☐ Jurat
☐ Oath/Affirmation   ☐ Certification
☐ Other: _____   Document Date: _____
Document Type: _____

Individual

Printed Name:	
Address:	
Phone # / Email: _____ _____	
Signature:	

Identification	Witness #1
☐ Individual ☐ Credible Witness	Printed Name:
☐ Known Personally ☐ Passport ☐ Driver's License ☐ ID Card Other: _____ ID #: _____ Issued by: _____ Issued On: _____ Expires: _____	Address:
	Phone or Email:
	Signature:

Identification (cont.)	Witness #2
	Printed Name:
Thumbprint Thumbprint	Address:
	Phone or Email:
	Signature:

Notary Entry #126

Date/Time:	____/____/_____ ____ am / pm
Location:	
Fee: $_____	Travel: _____

Type of Service

☐ Acknowledgment   ☐ Jurat
☐ Oath/Affirmation   ☐ Certification
☐ Other: _____   Document Date: _____
Document Type: _____

Individual Signing

Printed Name:	
Address:	
Phone # / Email:	_____ _____
Signature:	

Identification	Witness #1
☐ Individual ☐ Credible Witness	Printed Name:
☐ Known Personally ☐ Passport ☐ Driver's License ☐ ID Card Other: _____	Address:
ID #: _____ Issued by: _____ Issued On: _____ Expires: _____	Phone or Email: Signature:

		Witness #2
Thumbprint	Thumbprint	Printed Name:
		Address:
		Phone or Email:
		Signature:

Notary Entry #127

Date/Time:	___/___/_____ ____ am / pm
Location:	

Fee: $_____   Travel: _____

Type of Service

☐ Acknowledgment   ☐ Jurat
☐ Oath/Affirmation   ☐ Certification
☐ Other: _____   Document Date: _____
Document Type: _____

Individual

Printed Name:	
Address:	

Phone # / Email: _____ _____

Signature:

Identification	Witness #1

Identification

☐ Individual   ☐ Credible Witness
☐ Known Personally ☐ Passport
☐ Driver's License ☐ ID Card
    Other: _____
ID #: _____
Issued by: _____
Issued On: _____
Expires: _____

Witness #1

Printed Name:
Address:

Phone or Email:
Signature:

Witness #2

Printed Name:
Address:

Phone or Email:
Signature:

Thumbprint	Thumbprint

Notary Entry #128

Date/Time:	_____/_____/_____ _____ am / pm
Location:	
Fee: $_____ Travel: _____	

Type of Service

☐ Acknowledgment   ☐ Jurat
☐ Oath/Affirmation   ☐ Certification
☐ Other: _____   Document Date: _____
Document Type: _____

Individual Signing

Printed Name:	
Address:	
Phone # / Email: _____ _____	
Signature:	

Identification	Witness #1
☐ Individual ☐ Credible Witness	Printed Name:
☐ Known Personally ☐ Passport ☐ Driver's License ☐ ID Card Other: _____	Address:
ID #: _____	Phone or Email:
Issued by: _____ Issued On: _____ Expires: _____	Signature:

		Witness #2
Thumbprint	Thumbprint	Printed Name:
		Address:
		Phone or Email:
		Signature:

Notary Entry #129

Date/Time:	_____/_____/_____ _____ am / pm
Location:	
Fee: $_____	Travel: _____

Type of Service

☐ Acknowledgment   ☐ Jurat

☐ Oath/Affirmation   ☐ Certification

☐ Other: _____   Document Date: _____

Document Type: _____

Individual

Printed Name:	
Address:	
Phone # / Email:	_____ _____
Signature:	

Identification	Witness #1
☐ Individual ☐ Credible Witness	Printed Name:
☐ Known Personally ☐ Passport	Address:
☐ Driver's License ☐ ID Card	
Other: _____	
ID #: _____	Phone or Email:
Issued by: _____	
Issued On: _____	Signature:
Expires: _____	Witness #2
Thumbprint Thumbprint	Printed Name:
	Address:
	Phone or Email:
	Signature:

Notary Entry #130

Date/Time:	_____ / _____ / _____ _____ am / pm
Location:	
Fee: $_____	Travel: _____

Type of Service

☐ Acknowledgment　　　☐ Jurat
☐ Oath/Affirmation　　　☐ Certification
☐ Other: _____　Document Date: _____
Document Type: _____

Individual Signing

Printed Name:	
Address:	

Phone # / Email: _____ _____

Signature:

Identification	Witness #1

☐ Individual	☐ Credible Witness	Printed Name:
☐ Known Personally　☐ Passport		Address:
☐ Driver's License　☐ ID Card		
Other: _____		
ID #: _____		Phone or Email:
Issued by: _____		
Issued On: _____		Signature:
Expires: _____		Witness #2

Thumbprint	Thumbprint	Printed Name:
		Address:
		Phone or Email:
		Signature:

Notary Entry #131

Date/Time:	_____ / _____ / _____ _____ am / pm
Location:	
Fee: $_____ Travel: _____	

Type of Service

☐ Acknowledgment   ☐ Jurat
☐ Oath/Affirmation   ☐ Certification
☐ Other: _____   Document Date: _____
Document Type: _____

Individual

Printed Name:	
Address:	
Phone # / Email: _____ _____	
Signature:	

Identification	Witness #1
☐ Individual ☐ Credible Witness	Printed Name:
☐ Known Personally ☐ Passport ☐ Driver's License ☐ ID Card Other: _____ ID #: _____ Issued by: _____ Issued On: _____	Address:
	Phone or Email:
	Signature:
	Witness #2
Thumbprint Thumbprint	Printed Name:
	Address:
	Phone or Email:
	Signature:

Expires: _____

Notary Entry # 132

Date/Time:	____/____/_____ ____ am / pm
Location:	

Fee: $_____   Travel: _____

Type of Service

☐ Acknowledgment   ☐ Jurat
☐ Oath/Affirmation   ☐ Certification
☐ Other: _____   Document Date: _____
Document Type: _____

Individual Signing

Printed Name:	
Address:	

Phone # / Email: _____ _____

Signature:

Identification	Witness #1

Identification	Witness #1
☐ Individual ☐ Credible Witness	Printed Name:
☐ Known Personally ☐ Passport ☐ Driver's License ☐ ID Card Other: _____	Address:
ID #: _____ Issued by: _____ Issued On: _____ Expires: _____	Phone or Email: Signature:

		Witness #2
Thumbprint	Thumbprint	Printed Name:
		Address:
		Phone or Email:
		Signature:

Notary Entry #133

Date/Time: _____/_____/_____ _____ am / pm

Location:

Fee: $_____   Travel: _____

Type of Service

☐ Acknowledgment   ☐ Jurat
☐ Oath/Affirmation   ☐ Certification
☐ Other: _____ Document Date: _____
Document Type: _____

Individual

Printed Name:

Address:

Phone # / Email: _____ _____

Signature:

Identification		Witness #1
☐ Individual ☐ Credible Witness		Printed Name:
☐ Known Personally ☐ Passport ☐ Driver's License ☐ ID Card		Address:
Other: _____ ID #: _____ Issued by: _____ Issued On: _____ Expires: _____		Phone or Email:
		Signature:
		Witness #2
Thumbprint	Thumbprint	Printed Name:
		Address:
		Phone or Email:
		Signature:

Notary Entry #134

Date/Time:	_____/_____/_____ _____ am / pm
Location:	
Fee: $_____ Travel: _____	

Type of Service

☐ Acknowledgment   ☐ Jurat
☐ Oath/Affirmation   ☐ Certification
☐ Other: _____   Document Date: _____
Document Type: _____

Individual Signing

Printed Name:	
Address:	
Phone # / Email: _____ _____	
Signature:	

Identification

☐ Individual   ☐ Credible Witness
☐ Known Personally ☐ Passport
☐ Driver's License ☐ ID Card
    Other: _____
ID #: _____
Issued by: _____
Issued On: _____
Expires: _____

Thumbprint	Thumbprint

Witness #1

Printed Name:
Address:

Phone or Email:
Signature:

Witness #2

Printed Name:
Address:

Phone or Email:
Signature:

Notary Entry # 135

Date/Time:	_____/_____/_____ _____ am / pm
Location:	
Fee: $_____	Travel: _____

Type of Service

☐ Acknowledgment   ☐ Jurat

☐ Oath/Affirmation   ☐ Certification

☐ Other: _____   Document Date: _____

Document Type: _____

Individual

Printed Name:	
Address:	
Phone # / Email:	_____ _____
Signature:	

Identification	Witness #1

		Printed Name:
☐ Individual	☐ Credible Witness	
☐ Known Personally ☐ Passport		Address:
☐ Driver's License ☐ ID Card		
Other: _____		
ID #: _____		Phone or Email:
Issued by: _____		
Issued On: _____		Signature:
Expires: _____		Witness #2

Thumbprint	Thumbprint	Printed Name:
		Address:
		Phone or Email:
		Signature:

Notary Entry #136

Date/Time:	_____ / _____ / _____ _____ am / pm
Location:	
Fee: $_____ Travel: _____	

Type of Service

☐ Acknowledgment   ☐ Jurat
☐ Oath/Affirmation   ☐ Certification
☐ Other: _____   Document Date: _____
Document Type: _____

Individual Signing

Printed Name:	
Address:	
Phone # / Email: _____ _____	
Signature:	

Identification	Witness #1

☐ Individual	☐ Credible Witness	**Printed Name:**
☐ Known Personally ☐ Passport ☐ Driver's License ☐ ID Card Other: _____		**Address:**
ID #: _____ Issued by: _____		**Phone or Email:**
Issued On: _____		**Signature:**
Expires: _____		**Witness #2**
Thumbprint	Thumbprint	**Printed Name:**
		Address:
		Phone or Email:
		Signature:

Notary Entry # 137

Date/Time:	_____/_____/_____ _____ am / pm
Location:	
Fee: $_____	Travel: _____

Type of Service

☐ Acknowledgment   ☐ Jurat
☐ Oath/Affirmation   ☐ Certification
☐ Other: _____   Document Date: _____
Document Type: _____

Individual

Printed Name:	
Address:	
Phone # / Email: _____ _____
Signature:

Identification	Witness #1
☐ Individual ☐ Credible Witness	Printed Name:
☐ Known Personally ☐ Passport ☐ Driver's License ☐ ID Card Other: _____ ID #: _____ Issued by: _____ Issued On: _____ Expires: _____	Address:
	Phone or Email:
	Signature:
	Witness #2
Thumbprint	Thumbprint	Printed Name:
		Address:
		Phone or Email:
		Signature:

Notary Entry #138

Date/Time:	_____/_____/_____ ____ am / pm
Location:	
Fee: $_____	Travel: _____

Type of Service

☐ Acknowledgment   ☐ Jurat
☐ Oath/Affirmation   ☐ Certification
☐ Other: _____   Document Date: _____
Document Type: _____

Individual Signing

Printed Name:	
Address:	
Phone # / Email: _____ _____	
Signature:	

Identification	Witness #1
☐ Individual ☐ Credible Witness	Printed Name:
☐ Known Personally ☐ Passport	Address:
☐ Driver's License ☐ ID Card	
Other: _____	
ID #: _____	Phone or Email:
Issued by: _____	
Issued On: _____	Signature:
Expires: _____	Witness #2
Thumbprint	Thumbprint	Printed Name:
		Address:
		Phone or Email:
		Signature:

Notary Entry #139

Date/Time:	____/____/_____ ____ am / pm
Location:	
Fee: $_____	Travel: _____

Type of Service

☐ Acknowledgment   ☐ Jurat
☐ Oath/Affirmation   ☐ Certification
☐ Other: _____   Document Date: _____

Document Type: _____

Individual

Printed Name:	
Address:	
Phone # / Email: _____ _____	
Signature:	

Identification	Witness #1
☐ Individual ☐ Credible Witness	Printed Name:
☐ Known Personally ☐ Passport ☐ Driver's License ☐ ID Card Other: _____	Address:
ID #: _____ Issued by: _____ Issued On: _____	Phone or Email:
Expires: _____	Signature:
	Witness #2
Thumbprint Thumbprint	Printed Name:
	Address:
	Phone or Email:
	Signature:

Notary Entry #140

Date/Time:	____ / ____ / _____ ____ am / pm
Location:	
Fee: $_____ Travel: _____	

Type of Service

☐ Acknowledgment ☐ Jurat
☐ Oath/Affirmation ☐ Certification
☐ Other: _____ Document Date: _____
Document Type: _____

Individual Signing

Printed Name:	
Address:	

Phone # / Email: _____ _____

Signature:

Identification	Witness #1
☐ Individual ☐ Credible Witness	Printed Name:
☐ Known Personally ☐ Passport ☐ Driver's License ☐ ID Card Other: _____	Address:
ID #: _____ Issued by: _____	Phone or Email:
Issued On: _____ Expires: _____	Signature:

		Witness #2
Thumbprint	Thumbprint	Printed Name:
		Address:
		Phone or Email:
		Signature:

Notary Entry #141

Date/Time:	_____ / _____ / _____ _____ am / pm
Location:	
Fee: $_____ Travel: _____	

Type of Service

☐ Acknowledgment   ☐ Jurat
☐ Oath/Affirmation   ☐ Certification
☐ Other: _____   Document Date: _____
Document Type: _____

Individual

Printed Name:	
Address:	
Phone # / Email: _____ _____	
Signature:	

Identification	Witness #1
☐ Individual ☐ Credible Witness	Printed Name:
☐ Known Personally ☐ Passport ☐ Driver's License ☐ ID Card Other: _____ ID #: _____ Issued by: _____ Issued On: _____ Expires: _____	Address:
	Phone or Email:
	Signature:
	Witness #2
Thumbprint	Thumbprint	Printed Name:

Thumbprint	Thumbprint	Printed Name:
		Address:
		Phone or Email:
		Signature:

Notary Entry #142

Date/Time:	_____/_____/_____ _____ am / pm
Location:	
Fee: $_____	Travel: _____

Type of Service

☐ Acknowledgment ☐ Jurat
☐ Oath/Affirmation ☐ Certification
☐ Other: _____ Document Date: _____
Document Type: _____

Individual Signing

Printed Name:	
Address:	
Phone # / Email: _____ _____
Signature:

Identification		Witness #1
☐ Individual	☐ Credible Witness	Printed Name:
☐ Known Personally ☐ Passport ☐ Driver's License ☐ ID Card		Address:
Other: _____		
ID #: _____		Phone or Email:
Issued by: _____		
Issued On: _____		Signature:
Expires: _____		Witness #2
Thumbprint	Thumbprint	Printed Name:
		Address:
		Phone or Email:
		Signature:

Notary Entry #143

Date/Time:	____/____/_____ ____ am / pm
Location:	
Fee: $_____	Travel: _____

Type of Service

☐ Acknowledgment   ☐ Jurat
☐ Oath/Affirmation   ☐ Certification
☐ Other: _____   Document Date: _____
Document Type: _____

Individual

Printed Name:	
Address:	

Phone # / Email: _____ _____

Signature:

Identification	Witness #1

Identification		Witness #1	
☐ Individual	☐ Credible Witness	Printed Name:	
☐ Known Personally ☐ Passport		Address:	
☐ Driver's License ☐ ID Card			
Other: _____			
ID #: _____		Phone or Email:	
Issued by: _____			
Issued On: _____		Signature:	

Identification		Witness #2	
Expires: _____		Printed Name:	
Thumbprint	Thumbprint	Address:	
		Phone or Email:	
		Signature:	

Notary Entry #144

Date/Time:	_____/_____/_____ _____ am / pm
Location:	
Fee: $_____ Travel: _____	

Type of Service

☐ Acknowledgment   ☐ Jurat
☐ Oath/Affirmation   ☐ Certification
☐ Other: _____   Document Date: _____
Document Type: _____

Individual Signing

Printed Name:	
Address:	

Phone # / Email: _____ _____

Signature:

Identification	Witness #1
☐ Individual ☐ Credible Witness	Printed Name:
☐ Known Personally ☐ Passport ☐ Driver's License ☐ ID Card	Address:
Other: _____	
ID #: _____	Phone or Email:
Issued by: _____	
Issued On: _____	Signature:
Expires: _____	**Witness #2**
	Printed Name:
Thumbprint Thumbprint	Address:
	Phone or Email:
	Signature:

Notary Entry #145

Date/Time:	_____/_____/_____ _____ am / pm
Location:	
Fee: $_____	Travel: _____

Type of Service

☐ Acknowledgment   ☐ Jurat
☐ Oath/Affirmation   ☐ Certification
☐ Other: _____   Document Date: _____
Document Type: _____

Individual

Printed Name:	
Address:	

Phone # / Email: _____ _____

Signature:

Identification	Witness #1
☐ Individual ☐ Credible Witness	Printed Name:
☐ Known Personally ☐ Passport ☐ Driver's License ☐ ID Card Other: _____ ID #: _____ Issued by: _____ Issued On: _____ Expires: _____	Address:
	Phone or Email:
	Signature:
	Witness #2
Thumbprint Thumbprint	Printed Name:
	Address:
	Phone or Email:
	Signature:

Notary Entry #146

Date/Time:	___/___/_____ ____ am / pm
Location:	
Fee: $_____	Travel: _____

Type of Service

☐ Acknowledgment   ☐ Jurat

☐ Oath/Affirmation   ☐ Certification

☐ Other: _____   Document Date: _____

Document Type: _____

Individual Signing

Printed Name:	
Address:	

Phone # / Email: _____ _____

Signature:

Identification	Witness #1

Identification

☐ Individual   ☐ Credible Witness

☐ Known Personally   ☐ Passport

☐ Driver's License   ☐ ID Card

    Other: _____

ID #: _____

Issued by: _____

Issued On: _____

Expires: _____

Witness #1

Printed Name:

Address:

Phone or Email:

Signature:

Witness #2

Printed Name:

Address:

Phone or Email:

Signature:

Thumbprint	Thumbprint

Notary Entry #147

Date/Time:	_____/_____/_____ _____ am / pm
Location:	
Fee: $_____ Travel: _____	

Type of Service

☐ Acknowledgment   ☐ Jurat
☐ Oath/Affirmation   ☐ Certification
☐ Other: _____   Document Date: _____
Document Type: _____

Individual

Printed Name:	
Address:	

Phone # / Email: _____ _____

Signature:

Identification	Witness #1
☐ Individual ☐ Credible Witness	Printed Name:
☐ Known Personally ☐ Passport ☐ Driver's License ☐ ID Card 　Other: _____ ID #: _____ Issued by: _____ Issued On: _____ Expires: _____	Address:
	Phone or Email:
	Signature:
	Witness #2
Thumbprint	Thumbprint	Printed Name:

Thumbprint	Thumbprint	Printed Name:
		Address:
		Phone or Email:
		Signature:

Notary Entry #148

Date/Time:	_____ / _____ / _____ _____ am / pm
Location:	
Fee: $_____	Travel: _____

Type of Service

☐ Acknowledgment ☐ Jurat
☐ Oath/Affirmation ☐ Certification
☐ Other: _____ Document Date: _____
Document Type: _____

Individual Signing

Printed Name:	
Address:	
Phone # / Email: _____ _____
Signature:

Identification	Witness #1

☐ Individual	☐ Credible Witness	Printed Name:
☐ Known Personally ☐ Passport		Address:
☐ Driver's License ☐ ID Card		
Other: _____		
ID #: _____		Phone or Email:
Issued by: _____		
Issued On: _____		Signature:
Expires: _____		**Witness #2**

Thumbprint	Thumbprint	Printed Name:
		Address:
		Phone or Email:
		Signature:

Notary Entry #149

Date/Time:	____/____/_____ ____ am / pm
Location:	
Fee: $_____	Travel: _____

Type of Service

☐ Acknowledgment   ☐ Jurat
☐ Oath/Affirmation   ☐ Certification
☐ Other: _____   Document Date: _____
Document Type: _____

Individual

Printed Name:	
Address:	

Phone # / Email: _____ _____

Signature:

Identification	Witness #1
☐ Individual ☐ Credible Witness	Printed Name:
☐ Known Personally ☐ Passport ☐ Driver's License ☐ ID Card Other: _____ ID #: _____ Issued by: _____	Address:
Issued On: _____	Phone or Email:
Expires: _____	Signature:

		Witness #2
Thumbprint	Thumbprint	Printed Name:
		Address:
		Phone or Email:
		Signature:

Notary Entry #150

Date/Time:	_____/_____/_____ _____ am / pm
Location:	
Fee: $_____	Travel: _____

Type of Service

☐ Acknowledgment   ☐ Jurat

☐ Oath/Affirmation   ☐ Certification

☐ Other: _____   Document Date: _____

Document Type: _____

Individual Signing

Printed Name:	
Address:	

Phone # / Email: _____ _____

Signature:

Identification	Witness #1

Identification

☐ Individual   ☐ Credible Witness

☐ Known Personally   ☐ Passport

☐ Driver's License   ☐ ID Card

    Other: _____

ID #: _____

Issued by: _____

Issued On: _____

Expires: _____

Witness #1

Printed Name:

Address:

Phone or Email:

Signature:

Witness #2

Printed Name:

Address:

Phone or Email:

Signature:

Thumbprint	Thumbprint

Notary Entry # 151

Date/Time:	____/____/_____ ____ am / pm
Location:	
Fee: $_____	Travel: _____

Type of Service

☐ Acknowledgment   ☐ Jurat
☐ Oath/Affirmation   ☐ Certification
☐ Other: _____   Document Date: _____

Document Type: _____

Individual

Printed Name:	
Address:	

Phone # / Email: _____ _____

Signature:

Identification	Witness #1
☐ Individual ☐ Credible Witness	Printed Name:
☐ Known Personally ☐ Passport ☐ Driver's License ☐ ID Card Other: _____ ID #: _____	Address:
Issued by: _____ Issued On: _____	Phone or Email:
Expires: _____	Signature:
	Witness #2
Thumbprint Thumbprint	Printed Name:
	Address:
	Phone or Email:
	Signature:

Notary Entry #152

Date/Time:	_____/_____/_____ ____ am / pm
Location:	
Fee: $_____	Travel: _____

Type of Service

☐ Acknowledgment   ☐ Jurat
☐ Oath/Affirmation   ☐ Certification
☐ Other: _____ Document Date: _____
Document Type: _____

Individual Signing

Printed Name:	
Address:	
Phone # / Email:	_____ _____
Signature:	

Identification

☐ Individual   ☐ Credible Witness
☐ Known Personally ☐ Passport
☐ Driver's License ☐ ID Card
   Other: _____
ID #: _____
Issued by: _____
Issued On: _____
Expires: _____

Thumbprint	Thumbprint

Witness #1

Printed Name:
Address:

Phone or Email:
Signature:

Witness #2

Printed Name:
Address:

Phone or Email:
Signature:

Notary Entry #153

Date/Time:	_____ / _____ / _____ _____ am / pm
Location:	

Fee: $_____   Travel: _____

Type of Service

☐ Acknowledgment   ☐ Jurat
☐ Oath/Affirmation   ☐ Certification
☐ Other: _____   Document Date: _____
Document Type: _____

Individual

Printed Name:	
Address:	

Phone # / Email: _____ _____

Signature:

Identification	Witness #1
☐ Individual ☐ Credible Witness	Printed Name:
☐ Known Personally ☐ Passport ☐ Driver's License ☐ ID Card Other: _____	Address:
ID #: _____ Issued by: _____	Phone or Email:
Issued On: _____ Expires: _____	Signature:
	Witness #2
	Printed Name:
Thumbprint Thumbprint	Address:
	Phone or Email:
	Signature:

Notary Entry #154

Date/Time:	_____ / _____ / _____ _____ am / pm
Location:	
Fee: $_____ Travel: _____	

Type of Service

☐ Acknowledgment   ☐ Jurat

☐ Oath/Affirmation   ☐ Certification

☐ Other: _____   Document Date: _____

Document Type: _____

Individual Signing

Printed Name:	
Address:	
Phone # / Email: _____ _____	
Signature:	

Identification

☐ Individual	☐ Credible Witness

☐ Known Personally   ☐ Passport

☐ Driver's License   ☐ ID Card

Other: _____

ID #: _____

Issued by: _____

Issued On: _____

Expires: _____

Witness #1

Printed Name:

Address:

Phone or Email:

Signature:

Witness #2

Printed Name:

Address:

Phone or Email:

Signature:

Thumbprint	Thumbprint

Notary Entry #155

Date/Time:	_____/_____/_____ _____ am / pm
Location:	
Fee: $_____ Travel: _____	

Type of Service

☐ Acknowledgment   ☐ Jurat
☐ Oath/Affirmation   ☐ Certification
☐ Other: _____   Document Date: _____
Document Type: _____

Individual

Printed Name:	
Address:	

Phone # / Email: _____ _____

Signature:

Identification	Witness #1
☐ Individual ☐ Credible Witness	Printed Name:
☐ Known Personally ☐ Passport	Address:
☐ Driver's License ☐ ID Card	
Other: _____	
ID #: _____	Phone or Email:
Issued by: _____	
Issued On: _____	Signature:
Expires: _____	Witness #2

Thumbprint	Thumbprint	Printed Name:
		Address:
		Phone or Email:
		Signature:

Notary Entry #156

Date/Time:	_____/_____/_____ _____ am / pm
Location:	
Fee: $_____	Travel: _____

Type of Service

☐ Acknowledgment   ☐ Jurat
☐ Oath/Affirmation   ☐ Certification
☐ Other: _____   Document Date: _____
Document Type: _____

Individual Signing

Printed Name:	
Address:	
Phone # / Email:	_____ _____
Signature:	

Identification	Witness #1
☐ Individual ☐ Credible Witness	Printed Name:
☐ Known Personally ☐ Passport	Address:
☐ Driver's License ☐ ID Card	
Other: _____	
ID #: _____	Phone or Email:
Issued by: _____	
Issued On: _____	Signature:
Expires: _____	**Witness #2**
	Printed Name:
Thumbprint Thumbprint	Address:
	Phone or Email:
	Signature:

Notary Entry #157

Date/Time:	_____/_____/_____ _____ am / pm
Location:	
Fee: $_____	Travel: _____

Type of Service

☐ Acknowledgment   ☐ Jurat
☐ Oath/Affirmation   ☐ Certification
☐ Other: _____

Document Date: _____

Document Type: _____

Individual

Printed Name:	
Address:	

Phone # / Email: _____ _____

Signature:

Identification	Witness #1

Identification

☐ Individual   ☐ Credible Witness
☐ Known Personally ☐ Passport
☐ Driver's License ☐ ID Card
   Other: _____
ID #: _____
Issued by: _____
Issued On: _____
Expires: _____

Witness #1

Printed Name:
Address:

Phone or Email:

Signature:

Witness #2

Thumbprint	Thumbprint

Printed Name:
Address:

Phone or Email:

Signature:

Notary Entry #158

Date/Time:	_____/_____/_____ _____ am / pm
Location:	
Fee: $_____	Travel: _____

Type of Service

☐ Acknowledgment   ☐ Jurat
☐ Oath/Affirmation   ☐ Certification
☐ Other: _____   Document Date: _____
Document Type: _____

Individual Signing

Printed Name:	
Address:	

Phone # / Email: _____ _____

Signature:

Identification		Witness #1
☐ Individual	☐ Credible Witness	Printed Name:
☐ Known Personally ☐ Passport		Address:
☐ Driver's License ☐ ID Card		
Other: _____		
ID #: _____		Phone or Email:
Issued by: _____		
Issued On: _____		Signature:
Expires: _____		**Witness #2**

Thumbprint	Thumbprint	Printed Name:
		Address:
		Phone or Email:
		Signature:

Notary Entry #159

Date/Time:	_____ / _____ / _____ _____ am / pm
Location:	
Fee: $_____	Travel: _____

Type of Service

☐ Acknowledgment   ☐ Jurat
☐ Oath/Affirmation   ☐ Certification
☐ Other: _____   Document Date: _____
Document Type: _____

Individual

Printed Name:	
Address:	

Phone # / Email: _____ _____

Signature:

Identification	Witness #1
☐ Individual ☐ Credible Witness	Printed Name:
☐ Known Personally ☐ Passport ☐ Driver's License ☐ ID Card Other: _____	Address:
ID #: _____ Issued by: _____ Issued On: _____	Phone or Email:
Expires: _____	Signature:

		Witness #2
Thumbprint	Thumbprint	Printed Name:
		Address:
		Phone or Email:
		Signature:

Notary Entry #160

Date/Time:	_____ / _____ / _____ _____ am / pm
Location:	
Fee: $_____ Travel: _____	

Type of Service

☐ Acknowledgment ☐ Jurat
☐ Oath/Affirmation ☐ Certification
☐ Other: _____ Document Date: _____
Document Type: _____

Individual Signing

Printed Name:	
Address:	
Phone # / Email: _____ _____	
Signature:	

Identification		Witness #1
☐ Individual	☐ Credible Witness	Printed Name:
☐ Known Personally	☐ Passport	Address:
☐ Driver's License	☐ ID Card	
Other: _____		
ID #: _____		Phone or Email:
Issued by: _____		
Issued On: _____		Signature:
Expires: _____		**Witness #2**
Thumbprint	Thumbprint	Printed Name:
		Address:
		Phone or Email:
		Signature:

Notary Entry #161

Date/Time: ____/____/_____ ____ am / pm

Location:

Fee: $_____ Travel: _____

Type of Service

☐ Acknowledgment   ☐ Jurat
☐ Oath/Affirmation   ☐ Certification
☐ Other: _____   Document Date: _____
Document Type: _____

Individual

Printed Name:

Address:

Phone # / Email: _____ _____

Signature:

Identification	Witness #1
☐ Individual ☐ Credible Witness	Printed Name:
☐ Known Personally ☐ Passport ☐ Driver's License ☐ ID Card	Address:
Other: _____	
ID #: _____	Phone or Email:
Issued by: _____	
Issued On: _____	Signature:
Expires: _____	**Witness #2**
Thumbprint	Thumbprint	Printed Name:

Thumbprint	Thumbprint	Witness #2
		Printed Name:
		Address:
		Phone or Email:
		Signature:

Notary Entry #162

Date/Time:	_____ / _____ / _____ _____ am / pm
Location:	
Fee: $_____	Travel: _____

Type of Service

☐ Acknowledgment   ☐ Jurat

☐ Oath/Affirmation   ☐ Certification

☐ Other: _____   Document Date: _____

Document Type: _____

Individual Signing

Printed Name:	
Address:	
Phone # / Email:	_____ _____
Signature:	

Identification	Witness #1

☐ Individual	☐ Credible Witness	Printed Name:
☐ Known Personally ☐ Passport		Address:
☐ Driver's License ☐ ID Card		
Other: _____		
ID #: _____		Phone or Email:
Issued by: _____		
Issued On: _____		Signature:
Expires: _____		

Witness #2

Thumbprint	Thumbprint	Printed Name:
		Address:
		Phone or Email:
		Signature:

Notary Entry #163

Date/Time:	_____/_____/_____ _____ am / pm
Location:	
Fee: $_____	Travel: _____

Type of Service

☐ Acknowledgment   ☐ Jurat
☐ Oath/Affirmation   ☐ Certification
☐ Other: _____   Document Date: _____
Document Type: _____

Individual

Printed Name:	
Address:	

Phone # / Email: _____ _____

Signature:

Identification	Witness #1

Identification		Witness #1
☐ Individual ☐ Credible Witness	Printed Name:	
☐ Known Personally ☐ Passport ☐ Driver's License ☐ ID Card 　Other: _____	Address:	
ID #: _____ Issued by: _____ Issued On: _____	Phone or Email:	
Expires: _____	Signature:	

Identification	Witness #2

Thumbprint	Thumbprint	Printed Name:
		Address:
		Phone or Email:
		Signature:

Notary Entry #164

Date/Time:	_____/_____/_____ _____ am / pm
Location:	
Fee: $_____	Travel: _____

Type of Service

☐ Acknowledgment   ☐ Jurat
☐ Oath/Affirmation   ☐ Certification
☐ Other: _____   Document Date: _____
Document Type: _____

Individual Signing

Printed Name:	
Address:	

Phone # / Email: _____ _____

Signature:

Identification	Witness #1

Identification

☐ Individual   ☐ Credible Witness
☐ Known Personally   ☐ Passport
☐ Driver's License   ☐ ID Card
    Other: _____
ID #: _____
Issued by: _____
Issued On: _____
Expires: _____

Witness #1

Printed Name:

Address:

Phone or Email:

Signature:

Thumbprint	Thumbprint

Witness #2

Printed Name:

Address:

Phone or Email:

Signature:

Notary Entry #165

Date/Time:	_____/_____/_____ _____ am / pm
Location:	
Fee: $_____ Travel: _____	

Type of Service

☐ Acknowledgment   ☐ Jurat
☐ Oath/Affirmation   ☐ Certification
☐ Other: _____   Document Date: _____
Document Type: _____

Individual

Printed Name:	
Address:	

Phone # / Email: _____ _____

Signature:

Identification	Witness #1
☐ Individual ☐ Credible Witness	Printed Name:
☐ Known Personally ☐ Passport ☐ Driver's License ☐ ID Card	Address:
Other: _____	
ID #: _____	
Issued by: _____	Phone or Email:
Issued On: _____	Signature:
Expires: _____	**Witness #2**
Thumbprint Thumbprint	Printed Name:
	Address:
	Phone or Email:
	Signature:

Notary Entry #166

Date/Time:	_____ / _____ / _____ _____ am / pm
Location:	

Fee: $_____   Travel: _____

Type of Service

☐ Acknowledgment   ☐ Jurat
☐ Oath/Affirmation   ☐ Certification
☐ Other: _____   Document Date: _____
Document Type: _____

Individual Signing

Printed Name:	
Address:	

Phone # / Email: _____ _____

Signature:

Identification / Witness #1

Identification

☐ Individual   ☐ Credible Witness
☐ Known Personally ☐ Passport
☐ Driver's License ☐ ID Card
   Other: _____
ID #: _____
Issued by: _____
Issued On: _____
Expires: _____

Witness #1

Printed Name:
Address:

Phone or Email:
Signature:

Witness #2

Thumbprint	Thumbprint

Printed Name:
Address:

Phone or Email:
Signature:

Notary Entry #167

Date/Time:	_____ / _____ / _____ _____ am / pm
Location:	
Fee: $_____	Travel: _____

Type of Service

☐ Acknowledgment   ☐ Jurat
☐ Oath/Affirmation   ☐ Certification
☐ Other: _____   Document Date: _____
Document Type: _____

Individual

Printed Name:	
Address:	

Phone # / Email: _____ _____

Signature:

Identification	Witness #1
☐ Individual ☐ Credible Witness	Printed Name:
☐ Known Personally ☐ Passport ☐ Driver's License ☐ ID Card Other: _____ ID #: _____ Issued by: _____ Issued On: _____ Expires: _____	Address:
	Phone or Email:
	Signature:

		Witness #2
Thumbprint	Thumbprint	Printed Name:
		Address:
		Phone or Email:
		Signature:

Notary Entry #168

Date/Time:	_____/_____/_____ _____ am / pm
Location:	
Fee: $_____ Travel: _____	

Type of Service

☐ Acknowledgment   ☐ Jurat
☐ Oath/Affirmation   ☐ Certification
☐ Other: _____   Document Date: _____
Document Type: _____

Individual Signing

Printed Name:	
Address:	
Phone # / Email: _____ _____	
Signature:	

Identification / Witness #1

Identification		Witness #1
☐ Individual	☐ Credible Witness	Printed Name:
☐ Known Personally ☐ Passport		Address:
☐ Driver's License ☐ ID Card		
Other: _____		
ID #: _____		Phone or Email:
Issued by: _____		
Issued On: _____		Signature:
Expires: _____		

Witness #2

Printed Name:	
Address:	
Phone or Email:	
Signature:	

Thumbprint	Thumbprint

Notary Entry #169

Date/Time:	_____/_____/_____ _____ am / pm
Location:	
Fee: $_____	Travel: _____

Type of Service

☐ Acknowledgment   ☐ Jurat
☐ Oath/Affirmation   ☐ Certification
☐ Other: _____   Document Date: _____
Document Type: _____

Individual

Printed Name:	
Address:	
Phone # / Email: _____ _____	
Signature:	

Identification	Witness #1
☐ Individual ☐ Credible Witness	Printed Name:
☐ Known Personally ☐ Passport ☐ Driver's License ☐ ID Card	Address:
Other: _____ ID #: _____ Issued by: _____ Issued On: _____	Phone or Email:
Expires: _____	Signature:
	Witness #2
Thumbprint Thumbprint	Printed Name:
	Address:
	Phone or Email:
	Signature:

Notary Entry #170

Date/Time:	____/____/_____ ____ am / pm
Location:	
Fee: $_____ Travel: _____	

Type of Service

☐ Acknowledgment   ☐ Jurat

☐ Oath/Affirmation   ☐ Certification

☐ Other: _____   Document Date: _____

Document Type: _____

Individual Signing

Printed Name:	
Address:	
Phone # / Email: _____ _____	
Signature:	

Identification	Witness #1
☐ Individual ☐ Credible Witness	Printed Name:
☐ Known Personally ☐ Passport ☐ Driver's License ☐ ID Card Other: _____ ID #: _____ Issued by: _____ Issued On: _____ Expires: _____	Address:
	Phone or Email:
	Signature:
	Witness #2
Thumbprint Thumbprint	Printed Name:
	Address:
	Phone or Email:
	Signature:

Notary Entry #171

Date/Time:	_____/_____/_____ _____ am / pm
Location:	
Fee: $_____	Travel: _____

Type of Service

☐ Acknowledgment   ☐ Jurat
☐ Oath/Affirmation   ☐ Certification
☐ Other: _____   Document Date: _____
Document Type: _____

Individual

Printed Name:	
Address:	
Phone # / Email:	_____ _____
Signature:	

Identification	Witness #1
☐ Individual ☐ Credible Witness	Printed Name:
☐ Known Personally ☐ Passport ☐ Driver's License ☐ ID Card	Address:
Other: _____ ID #: _____ Issued by: _____ Issued On: _____	Phone or Email:
Expires: _____	Signature:

		Witness #2
Thumbprint	Thumbprint	Printed Name:
		Address:
		Phone or Email:
		Signature:

Notary Entry #172

Date/Time:	_____ / _____ / _____ _____ am / pm
Location:	
Fee: $_____	Travel: _____

Type of Service

☐ Acknowledgment   ☐ Jurat
☐ Oath/Affirmation   ☐ Certification
☐ Other: _____   Document Date: _____
Document Type: _____

Individual Signing

Printed Name:	
Address:	
Phone # / Email: _____ _____	
Signature:	

Identification		Witness #1
☐ Individual	☐ Credible Witness	Printed Name:
☐ Known Personally	☐ Passport	Address:
☐ Driver's License	☐ ID Card	
Other: _____		
ID #: _____		Phone or Email:
Issued by: _____		
Issued On: _____		Signature:
Expires: _____		**Witness #2**

Thumbprint	Thumbprint	Printed Name:
		Address:
		Phone or Email:
		Signature:

Notary Entry # 173

Date/Time:	_____/_____/_____ _____ am / pm
Location:	
Fee: $_____	Travel: _____

Type of Service

☐ Acknowledgment   ☐ Jurat
☐ Oath/Affirmation   ☐ Certification
☐ Other: _____   Document Date: _____
Document Type: _____

Individual

Printed Name:	
Address:	

Phone # / Email: _____ _____

Signature:

Identification	Witness #1
☐ Individual ☐ Credible Witness	Printed Name:
☐ Known Personally ☐ Passport ☐ Driver's License ☐ ID Card Other: _____ ID #: _____ Issued by: _____ Issued On: _____ Expires: _____	Address:
	Phone or Email:
	Signature:
	Witness #2
Thumbprint Thumbprint	Printed Name:
	Address:
	Phone or Email:
	Signature:

Notary Entry #174

Date/Time:	_____/_____/_____ _____ am / pm
Location:	
Fee: $_____	Travel: _____

Type of Service

☐ Acknowledgment   ☐ Jurat

☐ Oath/Affirmation   ☐ Certification

☐ Other: _____   Document Date: _____

Document Type: _____

Individual Signing

Printed Name:	
Address:	

Phone # / Email: _____ _____

Signature:

Identification	Witness #1

Identification

☐ Individual   ☐ Credible Witness

☐ Known Personally   ☐ Passport

☐ Driver's License   ☐ ID Card

     Other: _____

ID #: _____

Issued by: _____

Issued On: _____

Expires: _____

Witness #1

Printed Name:

Address:

Phone or Email:

Signature:

Witness #2

Printed Name:

Address:

Phone or Email:

Signature:

Thumbprint	Thumbprint

Notary Entry #175

Date/Time:	_____/_____/_____ _____ am / pm
Location:	
Fee: $_____ Travel: _____	

Type of Service

☐ Acknowledgment   ☐ Jurat
☐ Oath/Affirmation   ☐ Certification
☐ Other: _____   Document Date: _____
Document Type: _____

Individual

Printed Name:	
Address:	
Phone # / Email: _____ _____	
Signature:	

Identification	Witness #1
☐ Individual ☐ Credible Witness	Printed Name:
☐ Known Personally ☐ Passport ☐ Driver's License ☐ ID Card Other: _____	Address:
ID #: _____ Issued by: _____ Issued On: _____ Expires: _____	Phone or Email:
	Signature:
	Witness #2
Thumbprint	Thumbprint	Printed Name:
		Address:
		Phone or Email:
		Signature:

Notary Entry #176

Date/Time:	_____/_____/_____ _____ am / pm
Location:	
Fee: $_____ Travel: _____	

Type of Service

☐ Acknowledgment   ☐ Jurat
☐ Oath/Affirmation   ☐ Certification
☐ Other: _____   Document Date: _____
Document Type: _____

Individual Signing

Printed Name:	
Address:	
Phone # / Email: _____ _____	
Signature:	

Identification	Witness #1
☐ Individual ☐ Credible Witness	Printed Name:
☐ Known Personally ☐ Passport ☐ Driver's License ☐ ID Card Other: _____	Address:
ID #: _____ Issued by: _____ Issued On: _____ Expires: _____	Phone or Email:
	Signature:
	Witness #2
Thumbprint Thumbprint	Printed Name:
	Address:
	Phone or Email:
	Signature:

Notary Entry #177

Date/Time:	____/____/_____ ____ am / pm
Location:	
Fee: $_____ Travel: _____	

Type of Service

☐ Acknowledgment ☐ Jurat
☐ Oath/Affirmation ☐ Certification
☐ Other: _____ Document Date: _____
Document Type: _____

Individual

Printed Name:	
Address:	
Phone # / Email: _____ _____	
Signature:	

Identification / Witness #1

Identification	Witness #1
☐ Individual ☐ Credible Witness	Printed Name:
☐ Known Personally ☐ Passport ☐ Driver's License ☐ ID Card	Address:
Other: _____ ID #: _____ Issued by: _____ Issued On: _____ Expires: _____	Phone or Email:
	Signature:

Witness #2

Thumbprint	Thumbprint	Witness #2
		Printed Name:
		Address:
		Phone or Email:
		Signature:

Notary Entry #178

Date/Time:	_____ / _____ / _____ _____ am / pm
Location:	
Fee: $_____	Travel: _____

Type of Service

☐ Acknowledgment   ☐ Jurat
☐ Oath/Affirmation   ☐ Certification
☐ Other: _____   Document Date: _____
Document Type: _____

Individual Signing

Printed Name:	
Address:	

Phone # / Email: _____ _____

Signature:

Identification	Witness #1
☐ Individual ☐ Credible Witness	Printed Name:
☐ Known Personally ☐ Passport	Address:
☐ Driver's License ☐ ID Card	
Other: _____	
ID #: _____	Phone or Email:
Issued by: _____	
Issued On: _____	Signature:
Expires: _____	**Witness #2**
	Printed Name:
Thumbprint Thumbprint	Address:
	Phone or Email:
	Signature:

Notary Entry #179

Date/Time:	_____/_____/_____ _____ am / pm
Location:	
Fee: $_____ Travel: _____	

Type of Service

☐ Acknowledgment   ☐ Jurat
☐ Oath/Affirmation   ☐ Certification
☐ Other: _____   Document Date: _____
Document Type: _____

Individual

Printed Name:	
Address:	
Phone # / Email: _____ _____	
Signature:	

Identification	Witness #1
☐ Individual ☐ Credible Witness	Printed Name:
☐ Known Personally ☐ Passport ☐ Driver's License ☐ ID Card	Address:
Other: _____	
ID #: _____ Issued by: _____ Issued On: _____	Phone or Email:
Expires: _____	Signature:

		Witness #2
Thumbprint	Thumbprint	Printed Name:
		Address:
		Phone or Email:
		Signature:

Notary Entry #180

Date/Time:	_____ / _____ / _____ _____ am / pm
Location:	
Fee: $_____	Travel: _____

Type of Service

☐ Acknowledgment   ☐ Jurat
☐ Oath/Affirmation   ☐ Certification
☐ Other: _____   Document Date: _____
Document Type: _____

Individual Signing

Printed Name:	
Address:	

Phone # / Email: _____ _____

Signature:

Identification	Witness #1
☐ Individual ☐ Credible Witness	Printed Name:
☐ Known Personally ☐ Passport	Address:
☐ Driver's License ☐ ID Card	
Other: _____	
ID #: _____	Phone or Email:
Issued by: _____	
Issued On: _____	Signature:
Expires: _____	Witness #2
Thumbprint Thumbprint	Printed Name:
	Address:
	Phone or Email:
	Signature:

Notary Entry #181

Date/Time:	____/____/_____ ____ am / pm
Location:	

Fee: $_____   Travel: _____

Type of Service

☐ Acknowledgment   ☐ Jurat
☐ Oath/Affirmation   ☐ Certification
☐ Other: _____   Document Date: _____
Document Type: _____

Individual

Printed Name:	
Address:	

Phone # / Email: _____ _____

Signature:

Identification	Witness #1

Identification

☐ Individual   ☐ Credible Witness
☐ Known Personally ☐ Passport
☐ Driver's License   ☐ ID Card
    Other: _____
ID #: _____
Issued by: _____
Issued On: _____
Expires: _____

Witness #1
Printed Name:
Address:

Phone or Email:

Signature:

Witness #2

Thumbprint	Thumbprint	Printed Name:
		Address:
		Phone or Email:
		Signature:

Notary Entry #182

Date/Time:	_____/_____/_____ _____ am / pm
Location:	
Fee: $_____	Travel: _____

Type of Service

☐ Acknowledgment   ☐ Jurat
☐ Oath/Affirmation   ☐ Certification
☐ Other: _____   Document Date: _____
Document Type: _____

Individual Signing

Printed Name:	
Address:	
Phone # / Email: _____ _____	
Signature:	

Identification	Witness #1

Identification

☐ Individual   ☐ Credible Witness
☐ Known Personally   ☐ Passport
☐ Driver's License   ☐ ID Card
    Other: _____
ID #: _____
Issued by: _____
Issued On: _____
Expires: _____

Witness #1

Printed Name:

Address:

Phone or Email:

Signature:

Thumbprint	Thumbprint

Witness #2

Printed Name:

Address:

Phone or Email:

Signature:

Notary Entry #183

Date/Time:	_____/_____/_____ _____ am / pm
Location:	
Fee: $_____ Travel: _____	

Type of Service

☐ Acknowledgment   ☐ Jurat
☐ Oath/Affirmation   ☐ Certification
☐ Other: _____   Document Date: _____
Document Type: _____

Individual

Printed Name:	
Address:	
Phone # / Email: _____ _____	
Signature:	

Identification		Witness #1
☐ Individual	☐ Credible Witness	Printed Name:
☐ Known Personally ☐ Passport		Address:
☐ Driver's License ☐ ID Card		
Other: _____		
ID #: _____		Phone or Email:
Issued by: _____		
Issued On: _____		Signature:
Expires: _____		Witness #2
Thumbprint	Thumbprint	Printed Name:
		Address:
		Phone or Email:
		Signature:

Notary Entry #184

Date/Time:	_____ / _____ / _____ _____ am / pm
Location:	
Fee: $_____ Travel: _____	

Type of Service

☐ Acknowledgment   ☐ Jurat
☐ Oath/Affirmation   ☐ Certification
☐ Other: _____

Document Date: _____

Document Type: _____

Individual Signing

Printed Name:	
Address:	

Phone # / Email: _____ _____

Signature:

Identification	Witness #1

Identification

☐ Individual   ☐ Credible Witness
☐ Known Personally   ☐ Passport
☐ Driver's License   ☐ ID Card
    Other: _____
ID #: _____
Issued by: _____
Issued On: _____
Expires: _____

Witness #1

Printed Name:

Address:

Phone or Email:

Signature:

Thumbprint	Thumbprint

Witness #2

Printed Name:

Address:

Phone or Email:

Signature:

Notary Entry #185

Date/Time: _____/_____/_____ ____ am / pm

Location:

Fee: $_____ Travel: _____

Type of Service

☐ Acknowledgment   ☐ Jurat

☐ Oath/Affirmation   ☐ Certification

☐ Other: _____   Document Date: _____

Document Type: _____

Individual

Printed Name:

Address:

Phone # / Email: _____ _____

Signature:

Identification	Witness #1
☐ Individual ☐ Credible Witness	Printed Name:
☐ Known Personally ☐ Passport ☐ Driver's License ☐ ID Card	Address:
Other: _____ ID #: _____ Issued by: _____ Issued On: _____ Expires: _____	Phone or Email: Signature:
	Witness #2
Thumbprint Thumbprint	Printed Name:
	Address:
	Phone or Email:
	Signature:

Notary Entry #186

Date/Time:	_____ / _____ / _____ _____ am / pm
Location:	
Fee: $_____ Travel: _____	

Type of Service

☐ Acknowledgment　　　☐ Jurat
☐ Oath/Affirmation　　　☐ Certification
☐ Other: _____　Document Date: _____
Document Type: _____

Individual Signing

Printed Name:	
Address:	
Phone # / Email: _____ _____	
Signature:	

Identification		Witness #1
☐ Individual	☐ Credible Witness	Printed Name:
☐ Known Personally ☐ Passport		Address:
☐ Driver's License ☐ ID Card		
Other: _____		
ID #: _____		Phone or Email:
Issued by: _____		
Issued On: _____		Signature:
Expires: _____		Witness #2
Thumbprint	Thumbprint	Printed Name:
		Address:
		Phone or Email:
		Signature:

Notary Entry #187

Date/Time:	_____/_____/_____ _____ am / pm
Location:	
Fee: $_____ Travel: _____	

Type of Service

☐ Acknowledgment ☐ Jurat
☐ Oath/Affirmation ☐ Certification
☐ Other: _____ Document Date: _____
Document Type: _____

Individual

Printed Name:	
Address:	
Phone # / Email: _____ _____	
Signature:	

Identification / Witness #1

Identification	Witness #1
☐ Individual ☐ Credible Witness	Printed Name:
☐ Known Personally ☐ Passport ☐ Driver's License ☐ ID Card Other: _____ ID #: _____ Issued by: _____ Issued On: _____ Expires: _____	Address:
	Phone or Email:
	Signature:

Witness #2

Thumbprint	Thumbprint	Printed Name:
		Address:
		Phone or Email:
		Signature:

Notary Entry #188

Date/Time:	____ / ____ / _____ ____ am / pm
Location:	
Fee: $_____	Travel: _____

Type of Service

☐ Acknowledgment   ☐ Jurat
☐ Oath/Affirmation   ☐ Certification
☐ Other: _____

Document Date: _____

Document Type: _____

Individual Signing

Printed Name:	
Address:	

Phone # / Email: _____ _____

Signature:

Identification	Witness #1
☐ Individual ☐ Credible Witness	Printed Name:
☐ Known Personally ☐ Passport ☐ Driver's License ☐ ID Card Other: _____	Address:
ID #: _____ Issued by: _____	Phone or Email:
Issued On: _____ Expires: _____	Signature:
	Witness #2
Thumbprint Thumbprint	Printed Name:
	Address:
	Phone or Email:
	Signature:

Notary Entry #189

Date/Time: _____/_____/_____ ____ am / pm

Location:

Fee: $_____   Travel: _____

Type of Service

☐ Acknowledgment   ☐ Jurat
☐ Oath/Affirmation   ☐ Certification
☐ Other: _____   Document Date: _____
Document Type: _____

Individual

Printed Name:

Address:

Phone # / Email: _____ _____

Signature:

Identification		Witness #1
☐ Individual	☐ Credible Witness	Printed Name:
☐ Known Personally ☐ Passport ☐ Driver's License ☐ ID Card		Address:
Other: _____		
ID #: _____ Issued by: _____ Issued On: _____ Expires: _____		Phone or Email:
		Signature:

		Witness #2
Thumbprint	Thumbprint	Printed Name:
		Address:
		Phone or Email:
		Signature:

Notary Entry #190

Date/Time:	_____ / _____ / _____ _____ am / pm
Location:	
Fee: $_____ Travel: _____	

Type of Service

☐ Acknowledgment   ☐ Jurat
☐ Oath/Affirmation   ☐ Certification
☐ Other: _____   Document Date: _____
Document Type: _____

Individual Signing

Printed Name:	
Address:	

Phone # / Email: _____ _____

Signature:

Identification	Witness #1
☐ Individual ☐ Credible Witness	Printed Name:
☐ Known Personally ☐ Passport ☐ Driver's License ☐ ID Card Other: _____ ID #: _____ Issued by: _____ Issued On: _____ Expires: _____	Address:
	Phone or Email:
	Signature:
	Witness #2
Thumbprint Thumbprint	Printed Name:
	Address:
	Phone or Email:
	Signature:

Notary Entry #191

Date/Time:	_____/_____/_____ _____ am / pm
Location:	
Fee: $_____	Travel: _____

Type of Service

☐ Acknowledgment ☐ Jurat

☐ Oath/Affirmation ☐ Certification

☐ Other: _____ Document Date: _____

Document Type: _____

Individual

Printed Name:	
Address:	

Phone # / Email: _____ _____

Signature:

Identification	Witness #1
☐ Individual ☐ Credible Witness	Printed Name:
☐ Known Personally ☐ Passport	Address:
☐ Driver's License ☐ ID Card	
Other: _____	
ID #: _____	Phone or Email:
Issued by: _____	
Issued On: _____	Signature:
Expires: _____	Witness #2
Thumbprint Thumbprint	Printed Name:
	Address:
	Phone or Email:
	Signature:

Notary Entry #192

Date/Time:	_____ / _____ / _____ _____ am / pm
Location:	
Fee: $_____ Travel: _____	

Type of Service

☐ Acknowledgment   ☐ Jurat
☐ Oath/Affirmation   ☐ Certification
☐ Other: _____   Document Date: _____
Document Type: _____

Individual Signing

Printed Name:	
Address:	

Phone # / Email: _____ _____

Signature:

Identification	Witness #1
☐ Individual ☐ Credible Witness	Printed Name:
☐ Known Personally ☐ Passport	Address:
☐ Driver's License ☐ ID Card	
Other: _____	
ID #: _____	Phone or Email:
Issued by: _____	
Issued On: _____	Signature:
Expires: _____	**Witness #2**

Thumbprint	Thumbprint	Printed Name:
		Address:
		Phone or Email:
		Signature:

Notary Entry #193

Date/Time:	_____/_____/_____ _____ am / pm
Location:	
Fee: $_____	Travel: _____

Type of Service

☐ Acknowledgment   ☐ Jurat

☐ Oath/Affirmation   ☐ Certification

☐ Other: _____   Document Date: _____

Document Type: _____

Individual

Printed Name:	
Address:	

Phone # / Email: _____ _____

Signature:

Identification	Witness #1
☐ Individual ☐ Credible Witness	Printed Name:
☐ Known Personally ☐ Passport	Address:
☐ Driver's License ☐ ID Card	
Other: _____	
ID #: _____	Phone or Email:
Issued by: _____	
Issued On: _____	Signature:
Expires: _____	**Witness #2**
	Printed Name:
Thumbprint Thumbprint	Address:
	Phone or Email:
	Signature:

Notary Entry #194

Date/Time:	_____/_____/_____ _____ am / pm
Location:	
Fee: $_____	Travel: _____

Type of Service

☐ Acknowledgment   ☐ Jurat
☐ Oath/Affirmation   ☐ Certification
☐ Other: _____   Document Date: _____
Document Type: _____

Individual Signing

Printed Name:	
Address:	
Phone # / Email: _____ _____
Signature:

Identification	Witness #1
☐ Individual ☐ Credible Witness	Printed Name:
☐ Known Personally ☐ Passport ☐ Driver's License ☐ ID Card Other: _____	Address:
ID #: _____ Issued by: _____ Issued On: _____	Phone or Email:
Expires: _____	Signature:

		Witness #2
Thumbprint	Thumbprint	Printed Name:
		Address:
		Phone or Email:
		Signature:

Notary Entry #195

Date/Time:	_____/_____/_____ _____ am / pm
Location:	
Fee: $_____	Travel: _____

Type of Service

☐ Acknowledgment   ☐ Jurat
☐ Oath/Affirmation   ☐ Certification
☐ Other: _____   Document Date: _____
Document Type: _____

Individual

Printed Name:	
Address:	
Phone # / Email:	_____ _____
Signature:	

Identification	Witness #1

Identification		Witness #1
☐ Individual	☐ Credible Witness	Printed Name:
☐ Known Personally ☐ Passport ☐ Driver's License ☐ ID Card		Address:
Other: _____		Phone or Email:
ID #: _____ Issued by: _____ Issued On: _____ Expires: _____		Signature:

		Witness #2
Thumbprint	Thumbprint	Printed Name:
		Address:
		Phone or Email:
		Signature:

Notary Entry #196

Date/Time:	_____ / _____ / _____ _____ am / pm
Location:	
Fee: $_____ Travel: _____	

Type of Service

☐ Acknowledgment   ☐ Jurat
☐ Oath/Affirmation   ☐ Certification
☐ Other: _____   Document Date: _____
Document Type: _____

Individual Signing

Printed Name:	
Address:	
Phone # / Email: _____ _____	
Signature:	

Identification	Witness #1

Identification		Witness #1
☐ Individual ☐ Credible Witness	Printed Name:	
☐ Known Personally ☐ Passport ☐ Driver's License ☐ ID Card Other: _____ ID #: _____ Issued by: _____ Issued On: _____ Expires: _____	Address:	
	Phone or Email:	
	Signature:	
	Witness #2	
Thumbprint Thumbprint	Printed Name:	
	Address:	
	Phone or Email:	
	Signature:	

Notary Entry #197

Date/Time:	_____/_____/_____ _____ am / pm
Location:	
Fee: $_____	Travel: _____

Type of Service

☐ Acknowledgment   ☐ Jurat
☐ Oath/Affirmation   ☐ Certification
☐ Other: _____   Document Date: _____
Document Type: _____

Individual

Printed Name:	
Address:	

Phone # / Email: _____ _____

Signature:

Identification	Witness #1

Identification

☐ Individual   ☐ Credible Witness
☐ Known Personally ☐ Passport
☐ Driver's License ☐ ID Card
   Other: _____
ID #: _____
Issued by: _____
Issued On: _____
Expires: _____

Witness #1

Printed Name:

Address:

Phone or Email:

Signature:

Witness #2

Printed Name:

Address:

Phone or Email:

Signature:

Thumbprint	Thumbprint

Notary Entry #198

Date/Time: _____/_____/_____ _____ am / pm

Location:

Fee: $_____   Travel: _____

Type of Service

☐ Acknowledgment   ☐ Jurat
☐ Oath/Affirmation   ☐ Certification
☐ Other: _____   Document Date: _____
Document Type: _____

Individual Signing

Printed Name:

Address:

Phone # / Email: _____ _____

Signature:

Identification	Witness #1

Identification

☐ Individual   ☐ Credible Witness

☐ Known Personally ☐ Passport
☐ Driver's License   ☐ ID Card
   Other: _____
ID #: _____
Issued by: _____
Issued On: _____
Expires: _____

Thumbprint	Thumbprint

Witness #1

Printed Name:

Address:

Phone or Email:

Signature:

Witness #2

Printed Name:

Address:

Phone or Email:

Signature:

Notary Entry #199

Date/Time:	_____/_____/_____ _____ am / pm
Location:	
Fee: $_____	Travel: _____

Type of Service

☐ Acknowledgment   ☐ Jurat
☐ Oath/Affirmation   ☐ Certification
☐ Other: _____   Document Date: _____
Document Type: _____

Individual

Printed Name:	
Address:	

Phone # / Email: _____ _____

Signature:

Identification	Witness #1

Identification

☐ Individual   ☐ Credible Witness
☐ Known Personally ☐ Passport
☐ Driver's License ☐ ID Card
     Other: _____
ID #: _____
Issued by: _____
Issued On: _____
Expires: _____

Witness #1

Printed Name:

Address:

Phone or Email:

Signature:

Witness #2

Printed Name:

Address:

Phone or Email:

Signature:

Thumbprint	Thumbprint

Notary Entry #200

Date/Time:	_____/_____/_____ _____ am / pm
Location:	
Fee: $_____	Travel: _____

Type of Service

☐ Acknowledgment   ☐ Jurat
☐ Oath/Affirmation   ☐ Certification
☐ Other: _____   Document Date: _____
Document Type: _____

Individual Signing

Printed Name:	
Address:	

Phone # / Email: _____ _____

Signature:

Identification	Witness #1

Identification

☐ Individual   ☐ Credible Witness
☐ Known Personally ☐ Passport
☐ Driver's License ☐ ID Card
    Other: _____
ID #: _____
Issued by: _____
Issued On: _____
Expires: _____

Witness #1

Printed Name:
Address:

Phone or Email:
Signature:

Witness #2

Printed Name:
Address:

Phone or Email:
Signature:

Thumbprint	Thumbprint

Made in the USA
Las Vegas, NV
17 May 2023

72159384R00115